Swygert

Growing Up in the Middle of Nowhere in
a Little Town Nobody Ever Heard of

Jeffrey Harold Utterback

iUniverse, Inc.
Bloomington

Swygert
Growing Up in the Middle of Nowhere in
a Little Town Nobody Ever Heard of

iUniverse books may be ordered through booksellers or by contacting:

iUniverse
1663 Liberty Drive
Bloomington, IN 47403
www.iuniverse.com
1-800-Authors (1-800-288-4677)

Because of the dynamic nature of the Internet, any web addresses or links contained in this book may have changed since publication and may no longer be valid. The views expressed in this work are solely those of the author and do not necessarily reflect the views of the publisher, and the publisher hereby disclaims any responsibility for them.

Any people depicted in stock imagery provided by Thinkstock are models, and such images are being used for illustrative purposes only.

Certain stock imagery © Thinkstock.

ISBN: 978-1-4620-5455-8 (sc)
ISBN: 978-1-4620-5456-5 (hc)
ISBN: 978-1-4620-5457-2 (e)

Library of Congress Control Number: 2011916986

Printed in the United States of America

iUniverse rev. date: 10/25/2011

Dedication

This book is dedicated to my mother, Elsie Utterback, and in remembrance of my father, Dean Utterback. During my youth, I learned more from my parents than any book or classroom.

Contents

Preface

This book is a collection of stories about my childhood during the 1960s and 1970s in Swygert, Illinois. The stories are meant to be amusing, although they don't always have a well-defined plot. The characters in the book are my family members and my childhood friends and neighbors. The stories are true, but I certainly took liberties to embellish them and to fill holes in my memory. Although they quite often interrelate to each other, each chapter is intended to be a self-contained unit that may be enjoyed on its own. The chapters are not in any particular order. No attempt was made to indicate the chronological passage of time.

I was inspired to become a writer when I heard Bailey White reading an excerpt from her book, *Mama Makes up Her Mind*, on National Public Radio (NPR). I used her book as a model for my book, which I describe as a collection of humorous autobiographical essays. I am also a fan of David Sedaris, Sarah Vowell, and Garrison Keillor who also appear regularly on NPR and who's books may often be found in libraries shelved under Dewey decimal number 814: the essay section. Another influence, the *Seinfeld* television show, sometimes described as a show about nothing, taught me a very liberating philosophy. No plot? No problem.

Thanks to my friends and family for all the encouragement. Thanks to my wife, Susan, for all the support. Thanks to my daughter, Alyson, for adapting the cover art work. Last but not least, thanks to Aunt Martha for reading the manuscript and snickering in the appropriate places.

Introduction

~~~~~~

I grew up in the middle of nowhere, in a little town that nobody ever heard of, called Swygert, Illinois. During my childhood, Swygert consisted of eight houses, a cemetery, a junkyard, and a grain elevator. Counting every man, woman, child, cat, and dog, the population of Swygert was thirty-five.

My mom and dad moved to Swygert in 1962, two years before I was born. We remained in the same house all through my childhood, and my mom still owns the house at the intersection of the Swygert blacktop road and the gravel cemetery road, right across from the grain elevator.

My parents were born at the beginning of the Great Depression: my dad in 1929, and my mom in 1930. Their impressionable childhood years coincided with the worst economic time in U.S. history. The depression had a huge effect on them both. It taught them to be frugal, economical, thrifty, cautious, penny-wise, prudent, shrewd, sensible, and practical. The number-one goal for my parents was to avoid spending money, and they were very successful in that endeavor.

I'm sure my parents' attitude toward money had a bearing on their decision to buy the house we lived in. It was probably the cheapest house they could find, and the rural setting reminded them both of their own childhood. My mom grew up on a farm in southern Illinois, and my dad bounced around rural small towns in his youth.

When they bought the house in Swygert, my mom was an elementary school teacher, and my dad had recently completed training as a Linotype operator. (It's a machine used for typesetting in the printing industry.) My dad landed a job at a printing factory in Pontiac: a larger town not far from Swygert. That was the compelling reason for them to move up north. My mom got a teaching job also in Pontiac, and we became a two-income family, although you couldn't tell it from appearances.

Our house in Swygert was not a farmhouse, but it could be described as a farmette. We had a big yard with lots of trees and a big vegetable garden. There was an old chicken coop in the backyard that we used as a combination tool shed and catchall. The feature that stands out most in my memory is the doghouse. Well, we called it the doghouse because dogs lived in it, but it really was a dog kennel big enough to hold twenty or more dogs. It was a fully operational dog breeding business that was thrown in with the deal when my parents bought the house. Although they knew very little about dog breeding, my parents decided to have a go at it. They didn't want to pass up an opportunity to make more money.

When they moved into the Swygert house, my mom and dad had three daughters: Debbie, Joyce, and Jeny. I came along a few years later, and my little sister, Laura, came two years after me. We were a family of seven: mom, dad, four girls, and a boy. My dad and I were out numbered five to two.

There were several other families living in Swygert when I was young. The Hobarts were a family of seven with four boys and a girl. The Cagleys were just the opposite with four girls and a boy. Grandma Orr lived alone right next to her grandchildren in the Cagley house. There were also the Burtons, the Shockeys, the Webers, and the Baiers.

The Swygert blacktop road unfortunately served as the dividing line between two school districts; therefore, I couldn't attend school with my two best friends, Mike Hobart and Dale Cagley. The Hobarts and the Cagleys went to school in Saunemin, and the kids on my side of the road went to the Owego Elementary School.

I loved the Owego School, but I became aware that it was very unusual. It was a K-6 elementary school with an average of twenty-two students. I don't mean twenty-two students per class, I mean twenty-two students in the entire school! There were about three or four kids in each grade level. It seemed perfectly normal to me, but I later discovered that most schools have more than two teachers and one school bus! It wasn't a one-room school house. It was actually a very nice elementary school with a gym and a stage and a kitchen and a principal's office and a playground and two baseball diamonds and four classrooms and a water fountain. Two of the classrooms went unused because there weren't enough kids!

It's true that I grew up in a tiny town and attended a tiny school, but my childhood was anything but small. It was a rich childhood with all kinds of interesting experiences and adventures. My parents didn't see danger lurking around every corner, so my sisters and I were allowed vast amounts of freedom to learn and discover on our own. The stories in this book come from my memories of growing up in the middle of nowhere, in a little town that nobody ever heard of: Swygert, Illinois.

Country Gymnastics

We had a big, empty, brown, metal, fifty-five gallon drum in our yard. It was closed on both ends with only a small opening at the top. We always called it the barrel. The official purpose of the barrel was to act as the fulcrum for a teeter-totter. My dad laid the barrel on its side, placed a long wooden board over the barrel, and voila: instant teeter-totter. I used to play on the teeter-totter with my sister Jeny. Since she was older and heavier, we learned to place the board a little off center in order to even out the balance.

Jeny was four years older than I was and my closest sibling until Laura came along. The name on her birth certificate was Jenifer with one 'n', but everyone called her Jeny, and she always insisted on spelling Jeny with one 'n' as well. I'm sure this caused no end of confusion in school, and I think she still gets birthday cards addressed to *Jenny* even from close relatives. My mom says it wasn't a mistake. Her full name was purposely chosen to be Jenifer Lynn, because "four n's would just be too much." (But apparently, it was OK to have three.)

Jeny discovered the barrel could be used for other things besides just teeter-totter. She took the board off, and then, with the barrel still lying on its side, she tried to stand on it. It was quite a challenge. The metal was slippery, and I could see that it was hard for her to keep her balance. The barrel would roll out from under her, and she'd have to jump off. She didn't give up though. After some practice, she became pretty good at it, and then she started coaxing me to try it. Jeny was always much better at it than I was. She generally spent each summer going around barefoot, and I think her bare feet were well adapted for her barrel tricks.

After a while, just standing on the barrel was no challenge for Jeny. She decided to travel around the yard by rolling it under her feet like a lumberjack rolling a log. She called it, "walking the barrel." At first, she could only make it move a short distance before she fell off, but she kept trying, and she got better at it. Before long, she could walk the barrel a long way across the yard.

Jeny loved walking the barrel. She used to do it for hours at a time. When the neighbor kids came over, she showed them what she could do, and then each kid would have a go at it. We'd each take a turn to see how far we could walk the barrel. We put down sticks in the yard to mark the furthest. Jeny always won. She was the champion barrel walker of Swygert.

After a while, Jeny got so good at walking the barrel that she could go from one end of the yard to the other without falling off, but there was one place in the yard that was an extra special challenge. Our yard was generally flat, except for one spot where there was a small hump. Jeny took on this hump as her greatest barrel walking challenge. It was hard to control the speed on the downhill side of the hump, and it was almost impossible to stay on the barrel. Jeny tried it again and again. One time she finally made it over the hump, and she was so proud. She coaxed me to try it, but the hump was too difficult for me. I don't know if I ever succeeded in crossing the hump.

After Jeny mastered barrel walking, she looked for another challenge. We had a decorative, wooden fence all across our front yard. It consisted of vertical fence posts spaced every ten feet, and it had three horizontal boards all along its length. The whole thing was painted white. Jeny and I used to climb on the fence and sit on the top board and watch cars go by. One day, Jeny decided to try walking on the fence like a balance beam. It was difficult because the top board was about three feet off the ground, and it was only an inch and a half thick.

At first, Jeny steadied herself by holding onto the trunk of the big ash tree that grew next to the fence. It was no trouble for her to stand on the fence as long as she was near the tree, but trying to take a few steps away from the tree was difficult. I watched her try again and again. She kept losing her balance and having to hop to the ground and then try again. Just taking three steps away from the tree was a big achievement. I tried it too. It was difficult and a little scary. Three feet off the ground is pretty high for a little kid. When I felt myself losing balance, I'd hop to the ground and land on my feet. The alternative would have been painful.

Jeny spent hours walking on the fence and perfecting her skill. She'd steady herself with the tree and then slowing take a step away from the tree with her arms held out for balance.

After a lot of practice, she could actually take five or six steps after letting go of the tree.

Every ten feet along the fence, a fence post stuck up above the top board by about four inches. Those four inches proved to be quite an obstacle. The first time Jeny made it past the first fence post we both cheered. Of course, on the very next step, she lost her balance and had to hop off, but it was a great achievement. I think I finally got past the first fence post also, after a lot of practice and some good coaching from Jeny. At first, we challenged each other by counting to see who could take the most steps without falling off. This method of scoring proved to be rather dubious. We both began taking tiny steps in order to improve our score. In addition, when we felt ourselves begin to lose balance, we'd quickly take two or three more steps on the way down. After a while, we changed our scoring method to count distance rather than steps. That proved to be a better measure of success.

As the summer days went by, Jeny began saying that she wished she could walk the entire fence from end to end without falling off. I thought it was impossible. Neither of us had managed to walk more than a couple of fence posts. Jeny said she needed a lot of luck to do it. She began to search our yard for four-leaf clovers. She heard somewhere that they bring luck. Country folk don't bother to fertilize the yard, so we had plenty of dandelions and clover in amongst the grass. It was very easy to find three-leaf clovers, but it took a tremendous amount of searching to find a four-leaf one. I remember seeing Jeny hunched over a patch of clover slowly examining each one. I tried to help her with her quest, but my patience only lasted ten or fifteen minutes. Jeny had a longer attention span. After investing three or four hours, she actually found one. When she showed it to me, I examined it carefully to make sure that she hadn't glued an extra leaf onto a three-leaf one. It looked genuine to me, and I congratulated her. She carefully pressed it among the pages of her white Confirmation Bible that she received from the Odell United Methodist Church. Girls got white Bibles and boys got black ones.

The next day it rained in the morning, and the fence was a little slippery. Jeny thought that she should wait a few days for the good luck to take hold before making any more fence walking attempts. Instead of walking the fence, we started messing around in the ditch in front of our house. We were both barefoot, and I slipped on a little patch of mud. Jeny scoffed at me and called me a *Reject*, which was her favorite insult-of-the-month. I crossed my eyes, made a goofy face, and tried to look like a reject. It made Jeny laugh, and I liked to make her laugh. Jeny heard a car approaching, and she told me to do it again. Just as the car was passing our house, I stuck my heel in the mud, slid down the side of the ditch, and made a goofy face. Jeny yelled, *"REJECT!"* and pointed at me with both hands. The driver of the car turned her head and gave us a very strange look. We both thought that was hilarious. We spent the rest of the day doing it over and over again each time a car went past.

After a few days, when Jeny thought that the good luck from her four-leaf clover had sunken in, she decided to make another earnest attempt at walking the fence. I remember seeing some extra concentration on her face. There was something different about the way she approached the fence that day. She seemed to be absolutely determined to conquer the challenge. That four-leaf clover gave her a big boost of confidence. She began at the ash tree like always, and then, with both arms outstretched for balance, she began to slowly take steps along the top rail of the fence. She got to the first fence post and crossed over it. She kept going to the next fence post and crossed over it as well. I was amazed. I had never seen her do so well. She was making continuous balance adjustments, and she never looked down at her feet. She focused her eyes straight ahead. At one point, I saw she was close to falling, and I drew in a big fearful breath. Jeny scolded me with a loud "*SSSHHH*," but she kept her eyes focused like a laser beam straight ahead. She crossed over the third fence post and then the fourth. I kept my mouth shut tight, but I was mentally cheering as loud as my brain could cheer.

Jeny kept going and going. She was operating on the ragged edge of balance, making slow deliberate steps and quick continuous balance checks. When she came within grabbing range of the young maple tree near the other end of the fence, Jeny didn't hesitate to grab onto a branch as she walked by. For about two seconds, I wondered if using the maple tree was against the rules, but then I realized that there were no rules.

Jeny didn't want to leave the comfort of the maple tree, but she still had a few feet of fence left to go. She reluctantly let go of the branch and continued on. Step by step, she was determined to make it to the end. When she was within a few steps of the end of the fence, she knew it was in the bag. She threw caution to the wind, took three quick steps, and hopped down to the ground. I cheered and Jeny's face lit up. She looked at me and yelled, "Did you see that! I can't believe it! I made it! I made it!" I joined in with her celebration. We were both jumping up and down with glee.

We ran in the house to tell anyone who would listen. The first person we found was Mom. She was sitting at the kitchen table breaking a bucketful of green beans from the garden. We both were out of breath and trying to talk at the same time. We tried to tell Mom what happened and how amazing it was and what a tremendous achievement it was. Mom was confused. She didn't understand what all the excitement was about. Jeny told her that she found a four-leaf clover and, "It worked! It really worked!" Mom's face showed that she wasn't following us. I was still panting, but I made an attempt to help Mom understand. "It's true! I saw the four-leaf clover! She smashed it in her Bible!" Mom was having trouble connecting this four-leaf clover with the fence that we kept talking about. We finally managed to impress upon her that after an entire summer of trying, over and over, hundreds of times, Jeny had finally walked the entire fence from end to end. I told Mom that her daughter was the new undisputed champion fence-walker of Swygert.

I finally saw it register on my mom's face. She was starting to understand. As she broke off and discarded the rusty end of another green bean, Mom said, "You found a four-leaf clover," (we said "*Yes,*") "and it brought you luck," (we said "*Yes,*") "and you walked the fence from end to end." We said, "*Yes. Yes. Yes.*" Mom finally got it. We were sure that she'd be impressed with this amazing feat. We wanted her to laugh and shout and shower Jeny with congratulations. We wanted her to hoot and holler and jump for joy with us. We thought she might give Jeny a special treat or a reward for her accomplishment. Mom began to make a comment. Jeny and I watched her lips moving, as if in slow motion, as we anticipated her reaction. Then I felt all the blood drain out of my face. The only thing Mom said was, "You better stay off that fence. It's dangerous."

Owego School Etiquette

Although Owego School had three giant doors in the side of the bus garage, there was only one bus. One bus was perfectly adequate to pickup and deliver all of the kids, because the total student enrollment, for all six grades, never exceeded twenty or twenty-five at the most. The spare bays in the garage went unused, and gave the janitor vast amounts of elbow room for puttering with the lawnmower.

The janitor at Owego School was also the bus driver. He was very comfortable in his position performing his duties year after year. By the time I entered Owego School, he had already been working there for over twenty years, and I think he continued for another ten or fifteen after I was gone. His name was Ernie when we were on the bus, but it was Mr. Abraham when we were within earshot of the principal, Mrs. Shultz.

The entire bus route was about an hour long. It meandered all around the gravel roads near Swygert. The kids at the end of the route only had to ride a few minutes, but the unlucky ones at the beginning had a much longer ride. At one point, one of the parents made a *stink* about it during a PTA meeting, and after that, the bus route reversed direction every half year. We lived only a mile and a half from the school. At the start of the school year, when we were at the end of the route, I could wake up at 7:45, eat my Co Co Wheat's, and watch a half hour of *The Garfield Goose Show* before the bus arrived. After the Christmas break, my mornings weren't so leisurely, but aside from a little less sleep, I didn't really mind it terribly when the bus route was reversed. It was fun to be one of the first kids aboard and to ride the entire route and to greet each of my friends as the bus collected them one by one. Most of the kids were waiting patiently by their mailbox every morning when the bus arrived. All except for the Pulliam family. It was common for the bus to arrive at their house and find no one waiting. Ernie would stop the bus and blow the horn, then thirty seconds later the front porch door would fling open and three blonde headed boys would pile out of the house and sprint across the yard with coats half on and half off. As they climbed aboard the bus, I'd hear: "Sorry Ernie." … "Sorry Ernie." … "Sorry Ernie."

After collecting each child on the route, the school bus would arrive at school around 8:45 AM. All the kids would pile out and enter the school through the gym door. The school had a main entrance, but nobody ever used it. Everyone always entered through the gym. We'd all walk in an orderly fashion to our designated classroom. Mrs. Shultz didn't want to hear a lot of ruckus, so after being scolded a few times, we all learned to enter the school halfway quietly. All first-, second-, and third-graders entered the first classroom on the left. All fourth-, fifth-, and sixth-graders entered the first classroom on the right. The school had a total of four classrooms, but two of them went unused because there weren't enough kids!

When I was six years old, I began first-grade at Owego School. On the first day of school, I met the teacher that I'd have for the next three years. She was friendly and had a nice smile. She already had years of teaching experience under her belt, and she knew exactly what she was doing. She was patient and kind, but she could be firm when needed. Her name was Mrs. Wellenreiter, and I am very thankful for her, because she taught me how to read. Mrs. Wellenreiter was in charge of the primary grades, which included first, second, and third. She typically had no more than three or four kids in each grade level, which meant that during her most hectic years of teaching, she might have had a whopping total of a dozen smiling faces to teach.

When school got started on that first day, Mrs. Wellenreiter assigned the seats, and then all of the kids were anxious to tell her what exciting things they had done during the summer. Hands started going up all over the room, and Mrs. Wellenreiter patiently listened to the fascinating goings-on until we had exhausted our thoughts. About this time, Ernie walked into the room holding a giant wrench. It was tradition for him to adjust the desks on the first day of school each year. Mrs. Wellenreiter made sure to point out that Bryant Fraher, in the second-grade, had grown a few inches during the summer and needed to have his seat raised. After Bryant was comfortable, a few of the other desks were also adjusted, and then Ernie made one more look around the room before taking his leave.

When it was time to get down to business, Mrs. Wellenreiter instructed the second- and third-graders to organize their desks and get familiar with the text books that they would find inside. Then she started devoting her attention to the first-graders. She instructed us to open our desks and take out the *Dick, Jane, and Sally* book. I found a book with a picture of two girls and a boy washing a dog, and it matched the one that Mrs. Wellenreiter was holding up. Using the book, and a lot of good instruction from Mrs. Wellenreiter, I was actually able to read a sentence by recess time. "See Spot run." It was a proud moment for me.

Morning recess was at 10:00 AM for the first-, second-, and third-graders, then at 10:15, the fourth-, fifth-, and sixth-graders took their break. I didn't know how to read a clock when I began first-grade, but it didn't take more than a few weeks for me to learn what happened each day when the big hand was on the twelve, and the little hand was on the ten.

When the weather permitted, recess was outside. The outdoor playground had a lot of substantial equipment, and I was impressed. The swings had big, heavy seats made out of wood; not like those wimpy strap-type seats that they had at the Chautauqua Park in Pontiac. I climbed aboard one of the industrial-strength swings and enjoyed swooping fast and high. After a while, the slide caught my eye. It seemed to be as tall as the school. I liked climbing the ladder up to that thrilling height before whooshing down the polished metal on my butt. The deep dirt-hole, at the output of the slide, indicated many years worth of sliders had gone before me. After I had my fill of sliding, I went to the monkey bars. When I got to the top, I began to wonder why there were no rules against playing on this dangerous thing. Even at my young age, I perceived that a fall from the top could have dire consequences.

I talked to Bryant Fraher at the monkey bars. He was a big, friendly guy with a burr haircut, but he had a strange way of speaking. My mom had taught me to always be polite, but when I finally asked him why he talked so funny, he patiently explained to me that he had a stuttering problem. I made a mental note to ask my mom what that meant.

After recess, each and every kid stood in line at the water fountain to get a drink. Since I was new to this whole thing, I followed along with the crowd. I later learned that this was just a trick to make recess last longer. Every kid took a drink no matter if he or she was thirsty or not. It was an unwritten kid rule.

After recess, I began to understand the teaching process in Mrs. Wellenreiter's room. She'd devote slices of her time to each grade level, starting with the first-grade every morning, and then moving to the second-grade and then to the third. Before moving from one level to the next, she always made sure to assign some sort of task to keep the other two grades busy until the next time slice. As I was busy doing my little assignment, I could listen to what the other two grades were learning. The reading book for the second-graders was full of stories about the Pilgrims, so they also got a little history lesson along with the reading lesson. I enjoyed hearing about the Pilgrims and looked forward to next year. I wanted to have a look at the pictures to see Squanto, Miles Standish, and the Mayflower. When Mrs. Wellenreiter was conducting the math lesson with the third-graders, I heard strange and exotic words. I was very impressed when I heard them talking about numerators and denominators. Later in the year, I heard them saying things like, "ten to the fourth power" and "five to the third power." I wondered what this mathematical *power* was all about.

Lunchtime at Owego School was carried out in a very orderly manor. All of the kids lined up in the hall and waited their turn to receive a tray from the big window in the side of the kitchen. With very few exceptions, every kid in Owego School ate hot lunch. Mrs. Shultz frowned on anyone bringing a sack lunch, because it was such a shame to waste our beautiful kitchen and the nutritious food so graciously provided by the state of Illinois.

The cook at Owego School was Mrs. Abraham, Ernie's wife. She had a friendly smile, and she wore half glasses upon her nose which were connected to a chain around her neck. She only worked half days. She was free to go home after the pots and pans were washed. On the days when the state of Illinois commanded that celery sticks should be served, she made sure to fill them with peanut butter in order to help them go down. (Some of the kids just licked the peanut butter out.) Of course chocolate milk was included with each meal, (nobody ever drank the white stuff) and if your mom gave you two cents, you could buy an extra carton.

Mrs. Wellenreiter and Mrs. Shultz ate lunch right along with the kids. We all ate together at a long train of tables in the gym. It was a strict rule of Owego School etiquette that the kids were not allowed to sit down and start eating until the teachers sat down; and the teachers always went last in line. We all stood politely behind our chairs and when, at last, the teachers arrived with their trays, the gymnasium was filled with the sound of twenty steel folding chairs being pulled out and sat upon and scooted into eating position. During the meal, the kids were allowed to talk quietly, and the teachers conversed with each other. Once, when I saw Mrs. Shultz eating potato chips with a knife and a fork, I had no doubt who had started all these rigid lunchtime etiquette practices.

During my first three years at Owego School, when I was in Mrs. Wellenreiter's room, the school only had two teachers. Mrs. Shultz served double duty as the principal and also as a full-time teacher of the fourth-, fifth-, and sixth-graders. I was dreading my transition from third- to fourth-grade because of the stories that I heard about Mrs. Schultz. Somehow, the state of Illinois came to my rescue. During the summer prior to fourth-grade, my mom told me that Mrs. Shultz was being forced to devote at least a half day, everyday, to here principal duties; therefore, I'd only be subjected to Mrs. Shultz in the afternoons. Owego School was being honored with the addition of a new part-time teacher.

On the first day of fourth-grade, when the bus arrived at school with its cargo of farm kids, I got off the bus with everybody else, entered the gym door like usual, and walked down the hall; but for the first time in my life, I turned right to enter my classroom instead of left. The fifth- and sixth-graders seemed to know where to sit, and the new fourth-graders sat in the leftover desks.

When the teacher walked into the room, I felt like I had hit the jackpot. She was beautiful, and I fell instantly in love. I had a tingling feeling in my belly and a slight ringing in my ears. I didn't exactly know what was happening to me, but I liked it. When she began to speak to the class, I was even more delirious. I found that she had a positive attitude, a beautiful smile, and I could tell that she honestly cared about each and every one of us. She told us her name was Mrs. Eggenberger, and she was very happy to be our teacher; then she told us a little about her life. She lived in Pontiac and had two kids. Her husband was an executive at the Pontiac Savings and Loan. She told us that if we ever needed a pencil, we should just ask her, because she could get all the pencils that she wanted from the Savings and Loan for free!

Mrs. Shultz was slightly *put-out* by the whole thing. She didn't see any need to sit around in the principal's office every morning, but I suppose she eventually found something to keep her occupied: shuffling papers or something.

When lunchtime came, Mrs. Eggenberger broke all the rules. She went first in line instead of last. She took her tray to the table and sat right down and started eating. When she saw the kids standing patiently behind their chairs, she got an unsure look on her face, but she continued to eat. She awkwardly chit-chatted with whichever kid was standing beside her. I felt sorry that no one had clued her in. When the two veteran teachers arrived, and everyone sat down to eat, she looked a little more at ease. After lunch, Mrs. Eggenberger went home, and Mrs. Shultz took over teaching the fourth-, fifth-, and sixth-graders.

During the first month or two of school, I learned that Mrs. Eggenberger was what my dad would call, "a real go-getter." She was worldly, she wore stylish clothes, and she often attended professional sporting events with her husband in Chicago! She had the impression that the farm kids at Owego School were a bit backward. She was probably right.

Things started changing at Owego School. Somewhere, Mrs. Eggenberger found an unused equipment budget. She wanted us to broaden our horizons and play something other than softball and basketball. A set of field hockey sticks showed up one day, and she began teaching us the rules. A new climbing rope, which we had never had before, was installed in the rafters of the gym. She bought a football, over the objections of Mrs. Shultz, and taught us how to play using the two hand touch rules. She persuaded one of the fathers to build a wooden balance beam for P.E. Then, she imposed upon Mr. Abraham to install a volleyball net in the gym. This was very disturbing to Mrs. Shultz when she discovered that it would entail drilling holes into the walls.

During one of the PTA meetings, Mrs. Eggenberger suggested a field trip to the Brookfield Zoo in Chicago. Mrs. Shultz thought this was a terrible imposition upon Mr. Abraham to drive the bus in that horrible Chicago traffic! Some of the highways up there had three or four lanes going in each direction! But in the end, the PTA was charmed by Mrs. Eggenberger, and we got our trip to the zoo.

Google-Eyes

~~~~~~

In the summertime, it was standard operating procedure for every Swygert kid to practically live outside. We loved to be outside. There were trees to climb and swings to swing and BB guns to shoot and bikes to ride. There were kites to fly and baseballs to hit and dogs to play with and bugs to smash. Our parents gave us the freedom to go anywhere we liked as long as we stayed in Swygert. We rode our bikes or walked the short distance to our friend's houses. We gathered in one yard or another and played all day. Once in a while, someone would organize a baseball game.

It was quite normal for a kid to leave the house after breakfast and not be seen or heard from until called home for lunch. After wolfing down lunch just slowly enough to avoid the parental protests, each kid would once again disappear outdoors and not be seen or heard from until called home for supper. My dad had a special way of calling us home for supper. He whistled. He had a distinctive way of whistling which could be heard in all four corners of Swygert. When I heard his unique warbling whistle, I knew right away that it was my dad. I'd yell back, "Coooomiiiiiing!" Then I'd hop on my bike, hang my baseball glove on the handlebars, and zip home for supper. Each night after supper, the Swygert kids would once again leave their houses and wander outside to play in the cool of the evening. As the sun went down, you could hear parents calling their kids to come in. Everyone knew it was time to go home at sundown.

Sometimes my friends and I would get together with our Tonka Trucks and play *Elevator.* There was a big grain elevator right across the road from my house. It was the most prominent feature of Swygert. We noticed the daily goings-on at the elevator, and then we'd imitate the elevator process using our toy trucks and tractors. We had the whole elevator process well memorized. At harvest time, a farmer would pull up to the elevator driving a tractor and pulling a grain wagon. The farmer would drive across the big scale in front of the office and stop with his wagon on the scale. The elevator man in the office would write down the weight of the wagon and then flip a little switch to buzz the buzzer. I loved to imitate that noisy buzzer: "*KERRRRNNNNT.*" It could be heard all over Swygert.

When the farmer heard the buzzer, he'd drive his tractor forward into the elevator bay, and the elevator man would leave the little office to help unload the grain. Inside the elevator bay was a huge pit in the floor covered by a strong metal grate. The grate had hundreds of holes in it, and you could look down through the grate to see the pit below. The farmer would stop his tractor with the wagon full of grain positioned directly over the grate. The elevator man would open the door on the side of the wagon, and then all the grain would spill out into the pit below. While the grain was being dumped into the pit, there was a delicious sound similar to rain falling on a tin roof. Imagine a million tiny marbles falling into a giant metal pan.

Along with the sound, a great cloud of grain dust would rise up into the air.

There was an auger mechanism in the pit that would take all of the grain and *elevate* it up to the top of one of the grain bins. That's why they call it an *elevator*. After the wagon was empty, the farmer would drive his tractor back across the scale so that the empty wagon could be weighed. The elevator man would take another reading and then do the math to figure out the weight of the grain that was just delivered. The elevator man would hand a piece of paper to the farmer, and then the farmer would drive back to his farm for another load.

The grain elevator was managed by a short, fat man named Jack Nolan. Jack worked at the elevator eight hours a day. During the summer months, as far as I could tell, his job was to sit in the little office and swap stories with any farmer who happened to drop in. At harvest time, he became a lot more active, and the elevator would stay open late into the evening. The farmers would line up waiting for their turn to dump their grain.

One summer, we noticed a lot of excitement happening at the grain elevator. A construction crew had brought in cranes and tractors and scaffolding and ladders and cement mixers. The elevator was undergoing a major expansion project. They tore down the little wooden office shack and built a brand new office. They replaced the old scale, which was only big enough to weigh one wagon, with a huge new scale capable of weighing an entire semi truck. They also built two or three new grain bins, and those were *BIG* grain bins.

The construction crew showed up every morning, day after day and week after week. We could watch the daily progress as each new grain bin grew another five or ten feet taller. In the evenings, after the crew left, the Swygert kids were drawn to the construction site like bugs to a light bulb. We'd casually sneak over to the elevator hoping that no parents would take notice. If a parent did happen to see us, they would surely warn us to, "Get away from there!"

The construction men used a tractor for some of their work during the day. At quitting time they just turned it off and left it sitting wherever it happened to be. It was great fun for a kid to sit in the driver's seat of a real tractor. We'd grab the steering wheel and pretend like we were driving. Of course, it was mandatory to make those engine noises with your mouth: "Brrrrrooooooooommm."

The big tractor we played on was the kind of tractor that had a big scoop on the front. They called it a bucket tractor. The bucket ran on hydraulics. There were several levers used to move the bucket up and down, and to make it tilt when it was dumping its load. John Hobart was adventurous, and he instigated a lot of questionable tricks. Since he was four or five years older, we followed his lead even when we weren't so sure it was a good idea. Somehow, John taught himself to operate the levers on the tractor. He discovered that if the workmen left the bucket in the up-position, he could make it go down. Once the bucket was down, it was down for good. He couldn't make it go back up again without starting the engine. Of course, the workmen never left the keys, or I have no doubt that John would have been bold enough to start it up. Without the keys, John's bucket trick was a one-shot deal.

After supper, several kids would casually saunter over to the elevator property trying to avoid the eyes of any dish-washing moms who may happen to glance out the kitchen window. If we were lucky, the construction crew would have left the tractor bucket in the up-position: the higher the better. We'd climb up on the tractor and shinny up the bucket support arms until we were all standing or sitting in the actual bucket; then John would pull the lever, and we'd all have a short, one-way ride to the ground. This was big adventure! If our parents ever caught us, we'd have been skinned alive. It's even more fun when you know you shouldn't be doing it.

During the day, we noticed the different construction men doing their work. We often watched the progress from the safety of our own yards. After a while, we became familiar with the various faces of the men who returned to work each day. We never talked to the men, but we gave them nicknames amongst ourselves: Daredevil-Dan, Grouchy-Gus, Cigar-Guy, Hop-Along, Wide-Load, and old Mr. Red-Beard. There was also a young guy who was always spitting on the ground. We called him Snot-Boy.

My sister Jeny somehow developed a strong dislike for one guy who was there every day. He wore glasses with a heavy-looking, thick, gray frame. Jeny called him Google-Eyes. I'm sure she never talked to the guy, but she hated him anyway. Each day, when he showed up for work, Jeny would frown and say, "Oh no. Google-Eyes is back again."

I got the impression that Google-Eyes was some kind of supervisor. I used to see him unrolling papers and looking at charts and blueprints. At first, I didn't know why Jeny hated this guy, but then she told me that he ate his lunch in our yard every day. She was very sensitive to trespassing, and she took great offense that Google-Eyes would have the audacity to come across the road and sit under the tree that grew in the ditch in front of our house. It made her even more mad when she noticed that Google-Eyes was leaving his sandwich bags and candy wrappers on the ground. Jeny hated litterbugs even more than she hated trespassers, so Google-Eyes had two strikes against him: three, if you count those ugly glasses.

My mom tried to explain to Jeny that the ditch wasn't technically our yard, and that he was just looking for a shady spot to rest at lunchtime. That didn't cut any ice with Jeny. She continued to brood about it. Jeny got madder and madder as the litter began to pile up. One day she finally blew her stack and decided to take action. She waited until the evening when the work crew had gone home, then she gathered up a bunch of twigs and sticks and some other supplies, and she went to work.

On each piece of litter, Jeny placed two sticks in order to form a big X. She put an X on the banana peal and another X on each candy wrapper. She put a big X on the sandwich bags and every other piece of litter she could find. Then she made a little sign and tacked it to the tree so that Google-Eyes would be sure to see it the next day. The sign said, "Give a Hoot. Don't Pollute," then she drew a little picture of an owl. The owl was wearing glasses with a heavy-looking, thick, gray frame. The next day every single piece of litter was gone, and Google-Eyes never again ate his lunch in our yard. Chalk one up for kid power.

Grand Tour of the Doghouse

~~~~~~

When my parents bought our house in Swygert, it came with a fully operational dog breeding business. A building stood in the backyard that was specially built for the purpose. My parents always called it the doghouse, but it really would have been better described as a kennel. The building was heated in the wintertime and had electric lights and running water: cold only. Breeding stock also came with the deal. There were male and female Schnauzers, Cocker Spaniels, and Wirehaired Terriers. As the years went by, my parents decided to concentrate only on raising Schnauzers. The other breeds were slowly phased out.

The doghouse was a single story structure with a flat roof that slanted toward the back in order to shed the rainwater. All across the front of the building were seven separated dog-runs and seven little doggy doors that allowed the dogs to freely go in and out of the building. The dog-runs were divided from each other with wire fencing, and there were also separate dog pens on the inside of the building. The Schnauzers, Cockers, and Wirehair Terriers were kept separate from each other, and the males were kept separate from the females until the time was right. Across the back of the building were seven more dog-runs with seven more little doggy doors.

Each doggy door had a hinged wooden flap hanging down. The flap swung in both directions so the dogs could easily push their way in and out. I don't know if they pushed with their heads or with their noses, but it never impeded them. They seemed to love going back and forth, in and out, out and in. I can still remember the sound as the dogs passed through their little doggy doors, and the wooden flaps flapped back and forth: "Thawunk, squeak, squeak, squeak, squeak. Thawunk, squeak, squeak, squeak, squeak."

On the exterior of the building, right next to the human entrance door, there was an official looking sign that read, "OFFICE." I always imagined that someone should be manning the office, eight hours a day, waiting for a customer to show up, but that's not how it worked. Each time a new batch of puppies were ready to be weaned, my mom would put an advertisement in *The Pantagraph* newspaper which read something like, "Pure Bred AKC Miniature Schnauzer Puppies for Sale, $75," along with our phone number. People would call and tell us when they were coming, so there was no reason for anyone to actually man the office.

Just inside the door of the doghouse, there was an old wooden desk with a few papers laying on it and a whole lot of cobwebs. Above the old desk, there was a giant wall chart that showed the entire family tree of all the various dog breeds recognized by the American Kennel Club (AKC). Also hanging on the wall, was a dusty old calendar that never got updated. It was always December of 1966 in the doghouse. One time,

I flipped through the old calendar and found some writing on various pages. It said, "Serenade in Heat." A few days later it said, "Serenade Took." Some months later, "Serenade in Heat," then "Serenade Took." Apparently, Serenade was a very productive mother dog.

Next to the desk was a homemade doggy workbench. The workbench had clamped to it a black, metal, food grinder with a long crank handle. We used the grinder to grind up the dry adult dog food into puppy chow. When it came out of the grinder, it was about the consistency of sand. Of course, the newborn puppies lived on milk from the mother dog, but the puppies that were a few weeks old got the puppy sand. Sometimes we'd put a little water in the puppy sand, and then it looked a lot like those sand pies that kids make on the beach. The puppies loved it. The grinder had a funnel-shaped top where the adult dog food was poured in. We'd hold a puppy plate under the front side to catch the finished product. I loved when my mom let me crank the crank. That's big stuff for a little kid. The doggy workbench was used for other things too, like cutting doggy toenails, and cleaning out doggy ears, and also for one very unpleasant task that I'll save for later.

Next to the doggy workbench was a big metal cylinder with a lid on it. It was big enough to hold a big bag of Wayne's Dog Food. My mom always insisted that we put the lid back on the dog food because, "we wouldn't want to attract mice, now would we?" The dog food came in a fifty-pound bag. It was an orange-colored, tough-looking, paper bag that always felt a little greasy. There was some stitching at the top of each new unopened bag. We'd pull the stitching, and the whole top of the sack would open with a satisfying "zzzziiiiip."

Every so often, we'd make a trip into Pontiac to get another fifty-pound bag of Wayne's Dog Food at the Zehr's Hatchery. My mom must have determined that Zehr's was the cheapest place to get it. The guy at the hatchery would load it into the back of our Chevrolet Caprice Estate station wagon for free. That was a nice benefit because those bags were heavy, but when we got home, we were on our own. I'm not sure why a hatchery would sell dog food, but on the other hand, you can buy milk at a gas station, and you can buy motor oil at a grocery store, so go figure.

Another feature in the doghouse office was a great big sink with running water. It was very handy for giving dogs a bath. On the shelf next to the sink was the biggest bottle of doggy shampoo that I ever saw. It was in a clear glass jug, and the label was faded and streaked. That jug must have held two or three gallons of shampoo. During all the years that we were in the dog breading business, I never remember needing to buy any doggy shampoo. That big jug never ran out. I guess that's what you call a lifetime supply.

Just past the office is where the dogs lived. There were seven pens on the left and seven pens on the right with a walkway all down the center. When anyone walked down the walkway, the dogs would get excited and wag their tails and jump up and down. I'd always reach my hand over the pen and greet each dog. At the end of the walkway stood a big heater. The heater was made of brown metal with lots of holes in the side to let the heat out. At the top of the heater was a grate which we could lift up like opening the lid of a washing machine. Inside, we could see the big blue flame silently keeping the doghouse warm. At the back of the heater was a big stovepipe that went up and out to vent the smoke and fumes.

In the wintertime, when we were out playing in the snow, it was great to go inside the doghouse and greet all the dogs and then walk back to warm up near the heater. We'd take our gloves off and put them on top of the heater. If there was any snow on our gloves, we could hear little sizzling sounds as the snow warmed up, and the little water droplets fell into the big blue flame below. It didn't take long for our gloves to start steaming, and then we knew it was time to remove them. It was wonderful to put on my warm gloves after toasting them over the doghouse heater. Once, Jeny left her mittens on the heater a few seconds too long, and they got little brown scorch marks. They looked as if she had put them in a waffle iron.

The doghouse heater ran on some liquid that my dad called fuel oil. The fuel oil resided in a big tank next to the doghouse. Every so often, the FS man would come and refill the fuel oil tank. He drove a big white truck with a red FS logo on the side that stood for Farm Service. When he saw me, he'd always reach into the glove box and give me a candy sucker. While sucking on my sucker, I'd watch him do his work. He'd open the back of his truck, and I could see thick rubber hoses all coiled up. The FS man would choose the correct hose and then pull it over his shoulder until the hose began to unroll. At the end of the hose was a big nozzle with a trigger on it. The man would unscrew the lid to our tank, insert the nozzle, and pull the trigger. While this was happening, a rumbling motor at the back of the truck would indicate that the liquid was being pumped in. There was also a meter at the back of the truck with white numbers scrolling by. The rightmost digit on the meter showed 1/8, 1/4, 3/8, 1/2 etc. It whizzed by very quickly until the tank was full.

One time, my dad specifically asked me to come into the doghouse with him. He wanted to show me that a new batch of puppies was being born. He probably thought it was a good educational experience for me. He pointed out how each puppy emerged inside a little sack of goop. Then the mother dog would nudge and lick until the sack broke open. The puppies came into the world soaking wet with their eyes tightly closed. Their heads would wobble, and they would scoot around on their little legs. The mother dog would gently nudge them and coax each one to find a nipple. My dad always made sure to hook up the heat lamp whenever a new batch of puppies was born. The heat lamp kept the puppies nice and warm just like the fries at McDonalds.

When the Schnauzer puppies were only a few days old, an unpleasant task had to be undertaken. It was a characteristic of the Schnauzer breed to have a short stubby little tail. We were selling official AKC registered puppies; therefore, we had to dock the tails. When they thought I was old enough, my parents allowed me to witness this process. My dad would pick up a puppy and take it to the doggy workbench where my mom was waiting. The puppies were only a few days old, and they still had their eyes shut. In order to do the deed, my dad used a medium-sized, ordinary-looking pair of scissors. He'd hold up a puppy with one hand and cut off the tail with the other. The puppy would squeal and cry and wriggle around. Sometimes the puppy's eyes would pop open. I felt so sorry for them. Then my mom would apply alcohol and some kind of powder to stop the blood. For some of the puppies, my mom would use a special needle and thread to stitch up the wound. Usually, only one stitch was necessary. I was impressed with my mom's skills. She knew how to do stitches just like a doctor. After about thirty seconds the crying would stop, and my dad would give the puppy back to the mother dog for consolation.

When the puppies were a little older, Jeny would start begging Mom and Dad to let her play with them. She'd be allowed to take a few at a time out into the yard. It was good for the puppies to get used to being handled by humans. Of course, I always followed along to join in the fun. Jeny and I always took the puppies and sat under a big apple tree in the backyard. Jeny always told me that it was Debbie's apple tree: our oldest sister. I never knew why Debbie had a claim on it, but it didn't stop us from enjoying the tree. When we sat down on the ground, the puppies would go a little crazy and jump on us and lick our faces. We loved it.

When we were old enough to handle a shovel, Jeny and I were assigned a rather unpleasant task. Every few days we had to clean the dog-runs. First, we'd choose one of the bays, and we'd move the resident dogs out of that bay so we could work undisturbed. Luckily, the dogs always did their business in the outdoor dog-runs: never inside. I always wondered how the dogs knew to do it that way. We certainly never trained them to do it. I always imagined that the mother dogs would somehow pass on this knowledge to each new batch of puppies. In bark language she'd say, "Hey, don't do that in here. Go outside."

When performing this chore, we somehow decided that Jeny would be the scraper, and I'd be the scooper. Jeny used a long-handled, metal, spatula-shaped, tool to scrape the dog doo off the outdoor concrete slab. My dad called it an ice chopper, but we certainly didn't use it for chopping ice. I'd hold the big scoop shovel while Jeny used her tool to push the payload in. Then I'd carry the shovelful around to the backside of the doghouse and dump my load on the big pile of crap we had back there. It took about three or four shovelfuls to clean a dog-run, and then we'd rinse it down with a hose and move on to the next pen.

Sometimes I wondered why that big pile of crap didn't keep growing higher and higher each week. I guess it broke down and disintegrated on its own. Once in a while, my dad would actually light fire to the pile. If it was dry enough it would actually burn, and thick gray smoke would billow up into the sky. It smelled awful. I'm sure the other residents of Swygert really appreciated that.

Taking care of the dogs was a lot of work, but when you're raised with a dog kennel in your backyard then you don't know any different. Everyone in the family helped out. We gave them food and fresh water twice a day. Those water buckets were heavy, but I didn't mind helping with the twice-daily chore. Sometimes Jeny and I handled the evening feedings on our own. It only took ten or fifteen minutes to feed and water them all. We could have gone even faster, but Jeny insisted on personally talking to each dog and petting him or her a little bit.

One day, when Jeny and I were watering the dogs, we spilled some water on the sidewalk in front of the doghouse. We usually went barefoot in the summer. As I walked through the water, I left a few watery footprints. Jeny saw my footprints, and she became very concerned. She said, "You don't have an arch! You have flat feet!" I didn't know what she was talking about until she showed me a comparison. She walked through the spilled water and made a few footprints of her own. She said, "See! You're supposed to have an arch like mine!" She tried to impress upon me that having flat feet was a really bad thing. I was deeply concerned for about two seconds, then I shrugged my shoulders and went about my business.

The Science of Garbage Burning

When you live out in the country, there are no garbage trucks to pick up your trash. Country folks are forced to fend for themselves. Each family in Swygert had its own method for dealing with garbage. My family used the separation method. All of the glass bottles and tin cans would go into a special brown paper grocery bag under the sink in the bathroom. All of the paper and cardboard went into a special brown paper grocery bag under the sink in the kitchen. Using this method, we separated anything that would burn from anything that wouldn't. Of course, there were always a few questionable items. Do eggshells burn? Do banana peals burn? Do plastic milk jugs burn? If there was any doubt, I always dropped the questionable item in the burn sack. I never wanted to miss an opportunity to play scientist on trash burning day.

When my mom had a tin can to get rid of, she'd rinse it out thoroughly and then flatten it with her foot before dropping it into the non-burnable garbage sack. The rinsing helped to eliminate the smell. The flattening was purely for the sake of efficiency. She could fit a lot more cans in each sack if she flattened them out first. My mom was all about efficiency. The

Great Depression taught her to get the maximum amount of use out of everything: even free grocery sacks.

When the non-burnable garbage sack got full, we'd carry it out to the old chicken coop. There it would stay until we had collected a good truckload full of non-burnable garbage sacks, then my dad and I would load up the pickup truck and take a trip to the landfill. The little man in the landfill office charged a set price for a pickup truck, no matter if the truck was partially full or packed to the gills. This gave my dad a strong incentive to wait until the chicken coop was really full before taking a trip to the dump.

Sometimes I'd notice how other families in Swygert dealt with garbage. I was appalled to see that the Hobarts didn't separate cans from paper. They took sacks of mixed garbage out to their pile and lit a match to it. Of course, the glass bottles and tin cans didn't burn, but the labels did, so they were left with a nice big heap of rusty cans and blackened bottles in their backyard. I mentally scoffed at the Hobarts. Everyone knows that tin cans won't burn. I always assumed that my mom and dad did things the right way and any other way was the wrong way. We didn't have a heap of rusty cans in our backyard; we just had a heap of ashes, and I somehow thought that was better.

We burned our paper garbage in a special place in the yard that was designated for this purpose. The spot was demarcated by a crude three sided partition built out of concrete blocks. I suppose the idea was to keep the ashes contained in one spot and avoid having the wind blow the burning garbage all over the neighborhood. The concrete blocks stood there year after year. They were black after years of containing smoke and soot. The blocks weren't held together with mortar or cement. The only thing that held them together was gravity and friction and Newton's first law: an object at rest tends to stay at rest.

When I was old enough to light a match, my mom assigned me the job of burning the paper garbage. This was a task that needed to be done once or twice a week. I think I was about eight years old when I was assigned this task. People today would say eight is too young to allow a boy to light matches, but my parents taught me to be careful, and they had confidence in me. My mom didn't see danger lurking around every corner like some mothers do. I'm very thankful for her attitude. It allowed me to have a rich childhood full of discovery and adventure.

I enjoyed my garbage burning responsibility. It made me feel good to have a little chore. Every few days my mom would say, "The sack's getting full. Would you like to burn the garbage for me?" My mom always phrased her commands in the form of a question to soften the blow. I'd say, "sure," and grab a book of matches from the match drawer. We never actually bought matches. We got them for free, and we had a well-stocked drawer full. Every bank, store, insurance man, and auto mechanic, gave away matches as promotional material. On each matchbook cover was printed some advertisement for Emington Feed & Grain, or Graymont Coop, or Harley's Septic Tank Service: "A Flush Beats a Full House."

In winter or summer I'd take the brown grocery sack full of paper garbage out to the trash-burning place. If the wind was blowing, it might take four or five tries to light a match.

Once in a while, I'd get a crappy book of matches that wouldn't light at all. Those advertisers had no interest in actually making matches that worked. They just wanted you to read the stuff printed on the cover. After a while, I learned to always bring a backup book of matches in case I got hold of a dud.

My parents taught me to hang around and watch the garbage burn just to make sure that the wind didn't blow out the flame or blow a burning sack of garbage across the yard. Even if they hadn't have taught me that, I would have still hung around. I enjoyed watching the flames. There was something fascinating about it. I learned a lot from burning the garbage. That burn pile was like my own private science lab. I learned that newspaper burns poorly when it's all folded up, but if you feed in one sheet at a time, it burns like crazy. I learned that eggshells really don't burn, but they get black and smoke a lot. I learned that plastic doesn't exactly burn, but it melts in interesting ways. I remember watching the face of Mr. Clean on an empty plastic bottle. His face slowly distorted into strange shapes and finally melted into a little ball of goop.

My absolute favorite things to burn were plastic milk jugs. They were awesome. I'd take a big stick and put it through the handle of a jug, and then I'd hold the milk jug over the flames. At first, the bottom of the jug would smoke a little, and then it would start to get soft. After that, the plastic would catch fire and begin to burn slowly. Then the really cool thing would happen. As I stood there holding a flaming milk jug on a stick, little balls of flaming plastic would begin to drop to the ground. As each little flaming glob dripped off, it made a cool little sound: "pffffuuuuut … pffffuuuut … pffuut pffuut …

pffffuuuuut." I imagined myself to be some sort of giant super hero that could rain down flaming globs of molten lava onto the heads of the bad guys below. I started to look around for spiders and ants to torment.

Seven Pawns and a Checker

The main room of our house, where everybody hung out, was called the front room. My parents never called it the living room. It was always called the front room at the Utterback house. It was a nice big room with a huge floral area rug that only left about two feet of the wooden floor showing all around the edge. The TV was in the front room along with the davenport and three or four easy chairs. Next to my dad's favorite chair was an end table with a drawer. Upon the end table was a nice bright table lamp that he used when reading his *Popular Science* magazines. He loved reading about all those futuristic houses, cars, and airplanes.

Once, I found a little wooden box inside the drawer of the end table next to my father's chair. Even with my young eyes, I could tell that the wooden box was made with expert craftsmanship. It had a little door on the top that slid open to reveal the contents. Inside, I found strange looking black and white figures. I was very curious about them. Some of the pieces looked like little horses, but the rest of them were a complete mystery to me.

One cold and snowy December weekend, I asked my dad about the little wooden box. He told me the box was valuable, and that it had come all the way from overseas. He bought it when he was stationed in Germany during the Korean Conflict. He told me the pieces were used to play a game called chess. One of his army buddies had taught him to play the game. I got the impression that the boxful of chess pieces was a meaningful little treasure for my father. I liked board games, so I asked my dad if he'd teach me how to play. He told me to go get the checkerboard from the sun porch, and then we both sat down on the floor in the front room. Dad started setting up the strange looking pieces on the board. All the white ones were placed in two rows at one end of the board, and the black ones were placed at the other end.

Dad started by teaching me the names of the pieces: rook, knight, bishop, king, queen, and pawn. The black team also had one black checker, and the white team had one white checker. Then Dad taught me how each piece was allowed to move. "Bishops can only move on the diagonals," he said, "and rooks can only go vertically and horizontally, but queens can go anywhere they like." He also explained the strange pattern in which the horses were allowed to move, and he told me the horses should be called knights. After he explained how the pawns were allowed to move, I asked him about the checkers. He told me they were just the same as the pawns. My dad hated to waste words. To him, words were valuable, like money, and they shouldn't be spent frivolously. He only spoke when necessary. It wasn't necessary for me to know that two of the pawns had been lost, and that the checkers were being used as a substitute. Just as any child easily accepts Santa Claus as a fact, I simply accepted the fact that chess was played with seven pawns and a checker on each side. I never questioned it. That's just the way it was.

After telling me the rules, Dad said the best way to learn was just to plunge in and play a game; so we began. He told me that the white team always moves first, so I moved one of my white pawns forward two spaces. I expected my dad to immediately move one of his chess pieces, but he was in no hurry. He slowly picked up one of his pawns and moved it forward. After seeing his move, I immediately grabbed another one of my pawns and moved it ahead two spaces. Once again, my dad hesitated and stared at the board for a minute before making his move. We went back and forth like this moving our pieces. After I moved one of my bishops, Dad said, "Do you really want to do that?" I said, "Yeah, I guess so." Then he promptly captured my bishop. Ouch, that hurt.

As we continued playing, Dad tried to tell me that I shouldn't move so fast. He said that chess is a game that takes a lot of thought. After that, I started to deliberately let a little time go by before making each move. I pretended to be thinking, but I didn't actually use the time for thinking. I just mentally twiddled my thumbs until I thought that enough time had passed in order to make Dad happy.

I lost three or four games that weekend, but I didn't mind. Dad told me that it takes a long time to become a good chess player. I enjoyed spending time with my dad, and I really liked learning how to play chess. The more I played, the more fascinated I became with the game. In some ways, chess was like a war game with two armies facing each other on a well-defined battlefield. In some ways, chess was a mind game in which two smart guys mentally battled for supremacy. In some ways, chess was like *King Arthur and the Knights of the Round Table*, with foot soldiers, and cavalry, and royal kings and queens. Dad taught me that the king must always be respected and can never be captured, but if he is trapped, then the game is over. I thought that was cool for the king to have special privileges.

One time, I saw a chess set for sale in a store. There was something very strange about it. I saw eight pawns for black and eight pawns for white. There were no checkers. I pointed out the error to my dad, and he grinned at me. The time had arrived when it was necessary for me to know. He explained that two of the pawns from his chess set were lost in Germany, years ago, and that's why we used checkers. I was a bit stunned. I had no idea that we hadn't been playing with a regulation chess set. I lost some of my youthful innocence that day. It was as if he had told me that there was no Santa Claus; but I still thought the board in the store looked weird with eight pawns on each side.

Dad and I continued to play chess with his non-regulation chess set all throughout my childhood. We played more in the winter when life wasn't so busy. After a while, I finally learned the necessity for taking time to think before each move. I played much better when I considered each move carefully. Sometimes I'd get lost in my thoughts, and I was unaware of the passage of time. Dad would have to wake me from my trance. He'd say, "It's your move, isn't it?"

Each time I played chess, I learned something new and got better at it. Every time my dad said, "Are you sure you want to do that?" I used it as another learning opportunity. Year after year, as I grew older, I continued to play chess with my dad, and year after year, I continued to lose every game. My dad never let me win ... not even once ... and I appreciated that. I didn't want him to let me win. Each time I lost another game, I noticed myself improving, and my dad noticed it too. He'd say, "You gave me a heck of a game that time," or "You're getting hard to beat."

One time when I was in junior high school during Christmas break, my dad and I had a marathon chess session. We played seven or eight games on the same day. During one of those games, I actually won. I finally beat my dad at chess. He congratulated me. It was a sweet victory, and it was made even sweeter knowing that I had won fair and square. I didn't win because my dad let me win. I won because he had allowed me to learn and improve and progress over time. By never letting me win, my dad had given me a valuable gift: a gift that would keep on giving throughout the rest of my life. The gift taught me perseverance and self-reliance. The gift taught me how to stand on my own two feet in pursuit of a goal. But even now that I am a full fledged adult, and I have played thousands of chess games, each time I begin a game, I look down at my chess pieces standing ready in two straight rows, and there is a little voice in the back of my head that says, "Hey, where's the checker?"

Diamonds in the Ditches

One day, near the end of the school year, I was riding home on the bus and saw hundreds of telephone poles lying in the ditches. When I got home, my dad explained that the telephone company decided to modernize. They were taking down all the telephone poles in order to bury the cables underground. Apparently one work crew was responsible for taking down the poles, and another crew was responsible for removing them at some later date. There was a three- or four-week gap between the two events.

It was at this point in my life that I learned about the tremendous value of *insulators*. Insulators are little glass objects that were used to hold the telephone wire on the telephone pole. Since glass does not conduct electricity, it makes a good material to insulate. Screw threads were molded into the glass so they could be screwed onto wooden pegs connected to the cross members on each telephone pole. The adults in Swygert seemed to value the insulators as if there were diamonds in the ditches. The kids in Swygert were a bit puzzled by the whole thing. We saw no use for the little glass objects, but we soon jumped on the bandwagon. If your mom tells you that something is valuable, then it's valuable. I'd have never known that little pieces of green paper with dead presidents were valuable unless my parents taught me.

For a few weeks that spring, insulator collecting became a neighborhood obsession. It was common to see adults and kids walking along the ditches with brown paper grocery sacks gathering up all the valuable insulators they could find. I joined in with the collecting fad, and my mom was really into it as well. My dad thought the whole thing was a waste of time. He wasn't the kind of person to follow the crowd or to get caught up in fads. He was sensible and levelheaded. I admired him for that, but on the other hand, I think he missed out on a lot of fun.

There were several different insulator shapes and sizes. The dark brown ones were the most common type. They were plentiful and easy to find; therefore, they became the least desirable. After each family had two or three sacks full, nobody wanted the brown ones anymore. People started hunting for the other less plentiful colors. The insulator craze served as my introduction to the law of supply and demand. People tend to want things that are in short supply, and plentiful things are not sought after. I guess that's why dirt is dirt-cheap.

My mom had a special attraction to the green insulators. She said green glass was only made during the Great Depression. She was convinced that the green ones were made out of highly valuable *Depression Glass*. My mom spent a lot of time in her great quest for the precious green insulators.

At the very top of the desirability continuum were the highly prized transparent insulators. Most people called them white, but my dad insisted that we should always use the correct term for everything. He told me that if light can pass through something then it's not white; it's transparent. I tried to correct the other kids in the neighborhood when they kept calling them white. They just ignored me and told me I was weird.

The transparent insulators were big and heavy and very rare. It might take several hours worth of insulator hunting before finding a transparent one. After obtaining a few sacks full of brown ones and green ones, some people decided to hunt exclusively for transparent ones. They were highly desirable. Everyone wanted to find them. When a transparent one was found, it brought forth shouts of glee. After a few days, all of the transparent insulators near Swygert had been picked over, so I decided to expand the search on bicycle. I'd slowly ride for a mile or so in one direction and then ride back in the other direction. My eye was honed to detect the prized transparent insulators.

One day, while searching for insulators on my bike, I saw Jeny kneeling down in the middle of the Swygert blacktop road about a quarter of a mile away from home. The road was known as a tar and chips road. Jeny had found a little circular patch in the road that was mostly tar and no chips. It was a hot day, and the tar was soft. Somehow, Jeny got the idea to write a message in the tar. She grabbed a rock from the shoulder of the road and started writing. It was a nasty message about her enemy du jour: one of the Cagley girls that lived in Swygert. The next day I followed her back to the spot in the road, and I was surprised to see a different message in the tar. The original message was replaced with something nasty about Jeny. I was amazed that anyone else knew about her little patch of tar, and I was even more surprised that someone actually wrote a response. Jeny didn't seem surprised. She grabbed a rock and scribbled out the message in the soft tar. Then she got to work and wrote a new nasty message. When I asked her about it, she told me this had been going on for two weeks.

At some point, a rumor surfaced that the phone company wouldn't be happy with us taking all of their insulators. I never knew if it was true. As I walked along the ditches gathering insulators, I started to fear that every passing car contained telephone company police who were going to yell at me. I had visions of telephone men coming to my house and confiscating our grocery sacks full of insulators, but that never really happened.

It became a thing of pride for the women in Swygert to display their very best insulators in a prominent place. My mom put her prettiest ones in the kitchen windowsill so they could be seen from the road. When friends and relatives came to visit, they would "ooh and aw" over the insulators. Then my mom would tell them the story about how she found her favorite one stuck in the mud with a phone pole on top of it, and how she had to struggle to unscrew it from the peg that it was attached to.

When the telephone company finally came and picked up all the poles, the great Swygert insulator craze was over. Each family was happy in the knowledge that they had collected a treasure trove of insulators. Everyone assumed the insulators would appreciate in value over time. I heard the following phrase a thousand times: "Boy, these will really be worth big money someday!" No one ever defined how big was *big*, or when *someday* would occur. After the windowsills were full, people would generally stash the rest of them in basements or attics right along side the coffee can full of those valuable buffalo nickels. To this day, I suppose that if you spend some time in the basements and attics of Swygert, you will probably come across several long forgotten sacks of those tremendously valuable insulators.

Counting Down the Hits

Practically since the invention of the radio, there has been a big and powerful, fifty-thousand watt, clear-channel, AM radio station in Chicago known as WLS. The format has changed over the years, but when I was a kid, WLS played nothing but rock and roll hits twenty-four hours a day. WLS was the only station that anyone under the age of twenty-five listened to. My sister Jeny was no exception. She was quite a big fan of WLS. She knew the name of every DJ and could sing along with every song.

One year, a few days after Christmas, Jeny started talking about the big countdown that WLS was going to have on New Year's Eve. She said they would play the top one-hundred hits from the previous year in reverse order. She said at midnight they would play the number-one hit of the year. Jeny was excited about the countdown, and she got me interested in it too. We didn't really have any doubt that our parents would let us stay up until midnight, but we asked permission anyway just to confirm. We were both too young to have any New Year's Eve plans, so this was a big deal for us to look forward to.

When News Year's Eve arrived, the countdown began at 6:00 PM. Jeny had a radio in her bedroom and that's where we spent the evening listening to the hits. We listened to song after song in deep anticipation of hearing the number-one hit at midnight. While we listened, Jeny diligently kept a written list of each song that was played. She wrote down the title and the name of the artist. She had pre-numbered each line on several sheets of paper, and then she wrote down each song in reverse order. When the time came for her to take a bathroom break, she sternly warned me to keep track in case she missed the next one.

As the hours passed and the hits kept rolling along, Jeny decided to make use of the evening to decorate her bedroom. She found a box of old Christmas cards in the big hall closet. These were the cards that our family had received over the years from friends and relatives. She chose a few of her favorite cards and sat them upon her dresser and nightstand. Then she got some masking tape and began to attach Christmas cards all around her bedroom door-frame. She took a piece of masking tape and balled it up with the sticky side out, then she used a little ball of tape on the back of each card so it would stick on the wall. Her room began to look quite festive.

I made use of the time by working on my new plastic model car kit that I got for Christmas. My dad had introduced me to model building at a young age, and I was hooked on the hobby. Someone bought me a model of an old fashioned looking hot-rod truck. The picture on the box showed a bright yellow truck with an open truck-bed. The truck was all hopped up with slick tires and chrome exhaust. The back end of the truck was jacked-up as dictated by hot-rod fashion. In the truck bed were several old fashioned looking wooden barrels. On the side of the truck, it said, "Beer Wagon." The instruction sheet said that this truck was a hot-rod suds hauler. I thought the picture on the box was real cool, and I wanted to build the model to match the picture. I planned to carefully paint the little beer barrels brown with silver barrel hoops. I also planned to scuff up the slick tires with sandpaper to make them look authentic. I had begun building the Beer Wagon during the long Christmas break, and I decided to continue my work while listening to the big WLS countdown. I staked a claim on one area of the floor in Jeny's bedroom and laid down some newspaper. Then I brought in the box of model parts along with the necessary glue, paint, and paintbrushes. Of course, I also brought the instruction sheet that came with the model. My dad had taught me to diligently follow the instructions, step by step, when building a model. (I once helped one of my friends build a plastic model, and I was appalled to see that he didn't read the instructions.)

Jeny lit some candles to counteract the smell of the model glue, and we spent the frosty winter evening enjoying the rock and roll hits. As we listened hour after hour, the more popular songs began to be played. In the early evening, I didn't recognize some of the obscure hits, but as the night progressed, I found that I was familiar with every song. I remember hearing such unforgettable hits as *Frankenstein* by the Edgar Winter Group. I loved that drum solo in the middle of the song. I also remember hearing *Crocodile Rock* by Elton John, *Smoke On the Water*, by Deep Purple, and *Bad, Bad Leroy Brown*, by Jim Croce. (Aw yes, 1973 was quite a year for rock and roll.)

During the night, we each took breaks now and again to go downstairs for some peanut butter fudge or a Christmas cookie, but between us, we managed to keep Jeny's list of songs up to date. The disk-jockeys on WLS were very *hip* and *with it*. They announced each song and also threw in a snide remark or two. They had a habit of talking over the instrumental beginnings of each song, and then they would stop talking exactly at the point when the vocals began. They had the timing down to a science.

As it got closer to midnight, the anticipation increased. Jeny and I were just dying to know what the number-one hit song of the year would be. We began making predictions. I told her I thought the Tony Orlando song would be the winner, but my prediction proved false when I heard *Tie a Yellow Ribbon* about 11:30 PM. Jeny was rooting for *Killing Me Softly* by Roberta Flack, but that one was also played somewhere before midnight. They finally played the number-two song about 11:50 PM. After the song was over, we nervously waited for the DJ to announce number-one. Wouldn't you know it? The station started playing commercials just to increase the tension. Jeny and I sat through commercial after commercial. Each time another commercial came on, Jeny would frown and say, "Uh!" in a very disgusted tone of voice.

We watched the clock on Jeny's wall creeping toward midnight as if we could make it move by shooting brain waves at it. A watched pot never boils, and a watched clock never moves. When the minute hand finally made it to exactly 12:00, we heard the strains of a song beginning to play. The DJ said, "... and now here is the song you have all been waiting for. This is number-one."

The song was not familiar to me. I thought I'd recognize the opening chords, but I didn't. When the main vocal part began, I was still in the dark. It was a female voice, but I was alarmed that I didn't know the song. Was this some kind of joke? I never heard this song in my life! How could this be number-one? I looked at Jeny, and she seemed to know the song. As she made the final entry on her list, she was singing along like usual. The expression on her face indicated that she approved of this choice for the number-one hit song of the year.

I definitely did not approve. I was still completely perplexed. When the main chorus of the song came along, I heard the singer singing, "You're so vain. You probably think this song is about you." I couldn't believe it. It was the dumbest song I ever heard. What the heck does vain mean! Clouds in my coffee? … *Clouds In My Coffee??* How in the world did this goofy thing get to be number-one? I gave Jeny a bewildered look and asked in an alarmed tone of voice, "What in the heck is this?" Jeny just said, "Carly Simon … It's a good song."

I thought of all the hours I had expended listening to song after song and commercial after commercial and enduring all those hip comments from the DJ. I thought of how I had been dying to know the number-one song of the year, and when I finally found out, I wasn't familiar with it. I never heard the song before. It was such a disappointment. That was the day that I learned the true meaning of the word *anticlimactic*.

The Pole House

~~~~~~

When I was a child, I liked to follow my dad around on the weekends. I was always interested in what he was doing, and he was always doing something interesting: sharpening knives, pruning trees, tilling the garden, changing the oil in the lawn mower, or perhaps, if I was lucky, I could help him install a new flapper in the back of the toilet. (We had a lot of toilet flapper trouble.)

As I was following my dad around one day, I saw him load some big chains into the trunk of his old white Buick. I didn't dare ask what he was doing for fear of receiving a sarcastic remark. My dad didn't like to talk in general, and he especially hated answering questions from kids. He'd say, "Hey Jabber-box, why are you all the time asking questions?" I had found the safest thing to do was to keep my mouth shut and just follow, watch, and learn. I'd eventually find out what he was doing and sometimes he'd let me help.

We both got in the front seat of the Buick and dad turned on WBBM News Radio Seventy-Eight: the only station he ever listened to. We only drove a short distance down the gravel cemetery road when Dad stopped the car next to a telephone pole that was lying on the ground. The telephone company had recently decided to take down all the telephone poles and bury the cable. After pulling them out of the ground, they left the poles lying in the ditches for a few weeks until another crew came around to pick them all up.

Dad got out and opened the trunk. He started tying the chain around one of the phone poles. "You think that looks like a good one?" he asked. I said "Yep," and I began to realize that he was planning to drag this pole home behind the car. For about two seconds, I wondered if the phone company would mind; but I figured that my dad was operating on the old finders-keepers rule. Besides that, my dad never did anything wrong.

After the chain was attached to the pole at one end and to the Buick's bumper at the other, we got back in the car and drug the pole right into our backyard. Dad had a place picked out where he wanted to store the pole, right along side the doghouse with the other odds and ends that he kept there. I thought about trying to help him undo the chain, but I thought better of it. I waited until he actually indicated a need for help. After a few minutes, he made some grunts and hand motions, and then I helped him roll the pole closer to the doghouse. Words were somehow precious to my dad. He never wanted to waste any of them.

After storing the first pole, we went back for another and then another. I dutifully helped whenever Dad indicated a need for help. Some of the poles were stuck in the mud, but the Buick always managed to drag them home. I noticed that my dad was rather choosy about the ones that he wanted.

He seemed to like the very tallest and straightest ones with a minimal amount of rot.

I finally screwed up my courage to ask him what these poles were for. I was pleasantly surprised when he answered me with a minimal amount of sarcasm in his voice. He said, "Did you ever hear of a pole house?" I said no, and he took time to string a few sentences together so I could understand. He gave me the impression that a pole house is similar to a tree house. I pictured in my mind a little house way up high on the poles. He said the advantage of a pole house is that you don't harm any trees. After deciphering some more of my dad's cryptic words, I began to realize that this pole house was intended for me. It was to be a clubhouse for my friends and me. I think maybe I had asked him for a tree house at some time in the past, and this was his answer.

I was, of course, very happy about it. My imagination began to run with the idea. I loved building things, and I loved doing projects with my dad. This was going to be a father and son project, and I was thrilled. I was also thrilled with the prospect of having my very own pole house to show off to my friends; even though I still wasn't one-hundred percent sure what a pole house was. If it was anything like a tree house then I was happy.

Of course, I was raring to dive right in and begin the project. I asked my dad, "When do we start? Where do we build it? What's the first step?" My dad was in no mood to begin the project that day. He was a thinker. He was a planner. When he worked on a project, he liked to work nice and slow. He was a perfectionist. He hated making mistakes. His method to avoid mistakes was to go slow and think everything through one step at a time. He made it clear that we were not going to start the project that day, and I got the firm impression that I better not ask again.

Over the next two or three days, I thought about nothing else but the pole house. What does a pole house look like? How high will it be? How far can you see from up there? Will it have a ladder? Will it have a door? Will it have a lock on the door? Can I keep my sisters out? I was so sure that my Swygert friends would be envious. I planned to invite them up into my pole house after it was built. Maybe we'd start a club ... a pole house club ... a secret pole house club ... with no girls allowed.

I made frequent trips to the backyard to look at our poles. I began to feel proud of our poles. They were big and strong and long and straight. I walked on them like a lumberjack. I jumped on them. I pushed on them with my feet. I couldn't wait to make use of them. We had about six or seven of them, but Dad indicated that we only needed four for the pole house. When the time came, we'd pick out the best four for the purpose.

After a few days of trying to be patient, I couldn't wait any longer. I finally asked my dad, "When can we start the pole house?" I soon realized that I picked the wrong day to ask such a question: maybe even the wrong week or the wrong month. My dad was plagued with moodiness, and he was in another one of his moods. I saw the sarcasm fill his face. He looked at me and said, "Well go right ahead and start. Who's stopping you?" He knew I had no clue how to even begin the project, but that was his way of saying leave me alone.

I was disappointed, and I immediately left his presence. I knew the best thing to do was to stay away on the moody days. I went outside with my head hanging low. I walked around the backyard kicking dandelions, then I got a brilliant idea. My dad had just given me permission to start the project. He didn't mean it, but no one could deny what he said. It was in plain English. He said go ahead and start. I decided I'd take him up on that.

I went directly to the old chicken coop and grabbed a shovel. I spent about one minute thinking where to put my pole house, and then I began to dig. I figured the first step was to make four holes in the ground to stand-up the poles. The spot I chose was over next to the burn pile: the area where all the creeping-charlie had choked out the grass. I thought it was a nice place that wouldn't be in anyone's way. I picked a spot on the ground, and I started to dig. After all, my dad told me to go ahead and that's exactly what I did. I broke ground and continued to dig. I ran into some small roots, and I dug right through them. Digging is hard work for anyone and especially hard for a nine year old. After about ten minutes, I stopped to admire my hole. I bet it was at least six inches deep. I was proud of my hole. I was working up a sweat, and I was so glad that the project was finally underway.

My dad worked the second shift. He went to work every day around 3:30 PM. On his way to the Buick, he took a look in the backyard and saw me digging a hole. I think his attitude softened when he saw me working hard. He came over to have a look. He was quiet for a while as he looked over my progress. He didn't immediately reject my effort. I was dreading his reaction, but then my spirits lifted when I heard him say, "So this is where you want to put it, huh?" He stood and looked and thought and looked some more. As the seconds went by, they seemed like hours to me. It was just like waiting for a jury verdict at a murder trial. Finally he said, "Well, I think this spot will be OK." He looked at the plot of land that I had chosen. He said, "Yeah, I think this will work out." Then he said, "We better decide how big this thing is going to be." Of course, I had started so fast that it never entered my mind. He said, "Why don't we put each pole about eight feet apart, then the pole house will be an eight by eight square." That sounded fine to me. I didn't even know what a pole house was supposed to look like.

I was expecting him to go and get the dreaded tape measure and then spend the next several minutes measuring it all out. (Kids hate measuring. It takes all the fun out of it.) I was surprised to see him use an inexact method. My dad said, "I'm about six feet tall," and then he lay down on the ground with his feet at my hole. He said, "We'll put the next hole right about here," and he pointed to a spot on the ground above his head. We marked the spot by digging out a divot. Then he laid down three more times in order to rough-out the position of the four holes. After we had our four divots in the ground, I could visualize how big the pole house would be. It was a nice, sizable thing. I was pleased.

Before my dad left for work, he gave me one more suggestion. He told me the shovel I was using was not the proper tool for the job. I followed him out to the chicken coop, and he handed me a thing that he called a post-hole digger. I had seen it in there a hundred times, but I never knew what it was for. I thought it was a strange looking contraption. We walked back to my hole and dad showed me how to use the post-hole digger. He showed me how to slam the working end into the hole, and then I was amazed to see how the entire handle split apart like a giant pair of scissors. My dad split the handle open wide, and the two halves of the working-end closed like a clamshell. Using the tool, he pulled up some dirt and dropped it beside the hole on the ground. He used the tool three or four more times to make sure I understood how to use it, then he turned it over to me. He said, in order to make this pole house sturdy, each hole needed to be at least six feet deep. Then he said, "That'll keep you busy for a while," and he got in the Buick and went to work.

I started using the post-hole digger, and I became more comfortable with it after each stroke. It didn't move a lot of earth, but I could see how this tool was better suited for the task. I kept working for another hour or so, and I estimated that my hole was a foot and a half deep. I began to realize that these holes were going to take a lot of work. My mental time estimate for completing the job gradually lengthened. At first, I was planning to dig all four holes that day. As I kept working, I decided it would be good if I could finish just one hole that day. As the sweat rolled off my forehead, I began to think that I should call it a day when I got down to three feet. As my hands began to hurt, I started thinking maybe two feet would be a good goal to shoot for. It was definitely not a one-day job. That's why my dad was smiling as he left for work.

Over the next two or three days, I worked on the first hole. My sister, Jeny, took a slight interest in what I was doing, and she tried her hand with the post-hole digger. About ten minutes was enough for her. My little sister Laura also tried it, but she was too young and inexperienced to make any progress at all. Every time she lifted the digger up, all of her dirt dropped back into the hole. On Saturday, my dad took pity on me, and we took turns for a few hours. He was much more productive with the digger than I was. Strength and experience seemed to help a lot.

While my dad was helping me, we ran into tree roots. Tree roots are a devil to dig through. You have to slam the digger into the roots and try to cut through them. I hate tree roots. After the roots, we ran into clay. Clay is a devil to dig through. If you ever manage to bring up a scoopful, the clay sticks to the digger and generally slows down the whole process. I hate clay. About three feet down, we ran into rocks. Rocks are a devil to dig through. The digger hits a rock and it won't cut into the soil, and if the rock is very big, you can't bring it out. I hate rocks.

About four feet down, it became more difficult to use the post-hole digger. The sides of the hole prevented us from opening the two halves of the handle. The deeper we went the more difficult it was. The only hope was to dig the hole wider to enable us to continue the scissor action. Of course, it takes more time to dig a wider hole, and our progress was slowed even more. About five feet down, the post-hole digger became totally useless. The handle on the digger was only five feet long. When we slammed the digger into the hole for another scoopful, the entire digger disappeared below the surface. My dad realized that we couldn't go any further with that tool. If we were going to make it to the six-foot goal that he had set, we needed to think of something else. We quit work at that point with one five-foot hole to show for our efforts. My dad said he'd think about it, and he told me the other three holes would keep me busy.

I worked on my holes every day. Jeny helped me a little, and my dad also helped when he had time. As the days went by, I noticed my productivity improving. I was becoming a post-hole digging expert. My hands became callused, my technique improved, and my strength increased. I found that I could make a lot of progress even when working by myself. The post-hole digger began to feel like an old friend. I was becoming confident and adept. I knew what I was doing, and I knew my capabilities. It was very satisfying each time I pulled up a nice sizable amount of dirt. I'd slam the digger down into the hole and cut into the earth. I'd open the scissor handles and bring up a big satisfying scoopful. I'd drop the dirt beside the hole, and do the whole cycle over again. I got good at it, and it felt good to know that I was good at it.

After several more days, we finally had four respectable holes each five feet deep. The last three went faster than the first one. I really wanted to be done with digging, but I was worried about that final foot. I was dreading to find out how we were going to manage it. Dad stuck a tape measure down each hole and confirmed each one was five feet deep. Then he pondered a while. I could see his wheels turning. I was dreading what kind of torturous idea he'd come-up with to dig the final foot. Then I heard him say, "Well ... I think that's deep enough." I was so relieved. My spirits soared. We were finally done digging. Although I was very happy to be done with the post-hole digger, there was a bit of sadness as well. I was sorry to say goodbye to my old friend. It was like graduating from school: excited to move on but sad to leave.

The next step of the project was to put the poles into the holes. We used the old white Buick, once again, to drag four poles closer to the construction site. Somehow, we managed to up-end the first pole and drop it into its hole. We used brute, human, Utterback power to accomplish this. It took my dad and me and a few sisters as well.

After the first pole was in its hole, it leaned to one side because the hole was wider than the pole. My dad pushed it this way and that: testing, thinking, and wondering if the hole was deep enough. My dad went and got his level from the basement and held it up to the pole. He showed me that the little bubble in the green liquid would stay between the lines when the pole was perfectly plumb. My dad insisted that everyone around him should use the correct words when speaking. You check the *level* of a horizontal object, you check the *plumb* of a vertical object, and you will be ridiculed if you mix the two words up.

Dad told me to shovel some dirt in around the pole. (All that work digging holes, and now we were putting the dirt back in.) I started shoveling quickly. Dad told me to slow down. He said we needed to use a tamper. I never heard of a tamper. I thought it was just another one of his perfectionist ideas that would probably delay the progress. It turns out that a tamper is a fancy word for a two-by-four. We used the two-by-four to poke and pack down the dirt all around the pole. We shoveled in a little dirt and then tamp, tamp, tamp. We shoveled in a little more and then tamp, tamp, tamp. All the while, my dad was watching the bubble and leaning on the pole and keeping it plumb. I'd say, "Is it still level?" and he'd say in an annoyed tone, "No, but it's plumb." I could see that the pole was becoming firmer after each round of tamping. I grudgingly acknowledged that tamping was a good idea, but it was definitely a slow process.

After some more shoveling and tamping, the pole became firm, and it could stand on its own. My dad continued to check the *plumb* using his *level*, but it was OK. Eventually, we completed the job, and the first pole stood on its own: straight and tall and firm and, of course, plumb. The process was repeated for the rest of the poles, and before long, we had four majestic poles standing tall in our backyard. The pole house was progressing. The poles were done, and now all we needed was the house.

That summer I learned new words such as rim joist, floor joist, and lag bolt. I learned how to recognize the difference between a sixteen-penny galvanized nail, and a ten-penny cement coated sinker. I became friends with the hammer that my dad assigned to me. I felt like a big-shot when I put on my nail apron. I learned how important it was to have a pencil handy at all times. I learned the immense satisfaction of driving a nail straight on the first try. I learned how to leave the line, and how to measure twice and cut once. I also have fond memories of a little phrase that my dad always said after pounding the final nail into each board. "That ain't goin' nowhere."

When the time came to install the floorboards, I assumed we'd take a trip to the lumberyard and buy the necessary wood. I assumed wrong. My parents wouldn't dream of buying something that could be obtained for free. That's when I learned about skid-tops. Each time my dad said the word "skid-tops," I couldn't imagine what he was talking about. I saw a puzzled look on my mom's face as well. My dad was not the kind of guy to explain things, so we had to adopt the wait-and-see approach. I figured it out as time went by, and then I explained it to my mom. When paper was delivered at the printing factory where my dad worked, it came in a huge roll, and it was delivered on a wooden pallet known as a skid. There were piles and piles of these skids lying around at my dad's place of work, and they were apparently free for the taking. We chose the best ones we could find, and after we got the skids home, we tore them apart. We were only interested in the wider boards at the top of the skids, in other words, the skid-tops.

So, the floor of the pole house was made out of skid-tops. The skid-tops were attached to the floor joists. The floor joists were attached to the rim joists, and the rim joists were attached to the poles with lag bolts. After the floor was in place, it looked like a platform in the sky. The platform was about eight feet up in the air. That was a good, impressive, dangerous-looking height. I was pleased. I couldn't wait to show it off to my friends.

After the floor was in place, we built a railing all around the platform and left an opening in the railing for a door. The railing made me feel much more secure when I was up there. I was actually hoping for walls and a roof, but the summer was coming to an end, and my dad thought the railing would keep me happy until next year. He was right. I was very pleased with my pole house. It really looked more like an elevated deck than it did a house, but we still called it a pole house.

One day, before school started, my dad assigned me the task to paint the pole house. He said it was important to get a good coat of paint on it to protect the wood. He told me to put on some old clothes and come with him out to the garage. He opened up a gallon can of white, oil-based, FS (Farm Service) paint. He told me it was tough paint and would last a long time. He handed me the paint and a brush and said, "Go to it." I soon realized that I was on my own for this job. It was a bit scary to have the responsibility, but it also felt good to know that he trusted me. His only words of advice were, "Don't paint yourself into a corner." I actually consciously thought about his words when deciding where to start. I made sure not to start with the entrance. About two hours later, it was finished. There was a bright coat of white paint on the floor and the railing. Dad said there was no need to paint the poles because the creosote protected them. I took his word for it.

After I finished, I proudly told my dad that I was done. He marched me back to the garage and showed me how to wash out the brush. My dad's liquid of choice for cleaning paintbrushes was gasoline. He showed me how to swish the brush until the gasoline turned white, and then he'd find some weed in the yard to pour the white gas on. Dad told me that gas will kill just about anything, and we might as well kill some thistles and cockleburs.

After the brush was clean, it was time to clean me up. Dad poured a little gas on a rag and began to clean my hands and arms and knees and elbows. The paint came right off, and it felt good to be pampered and cared for, even if it was just a gasoline bath.

For a few weeks, I was content to use my dad's extension ladder to climb up into the pole house, but one day I got tired of carrying it in and out of the garage. I noticed some old tire chains hanging on a nail in the garage. They were all rusty, and no one ever used them, so I figured they were up for grabs. I installed the tire chains on my pole house, and they worked very well as a ladder. It reminded me of the rope ladders that I had seen at the circus. Another great feature is that my sisters weren't so keen to climb up the chain ladder. It actually increased my privacy, and I thought it was more rustic and masculine.

I used the pole house a lot after it was built. I spent time up there every day after school and listened to the mourning doves: "HooOOO Hoo...Hoo Hoo." I hooted back at them, and I was pretty good at it: "HooOOO Hoo...Hoo Hoo." I was convinced they thought I was another bird. The pole house was a great place to just stare out at the world and be alone with my thoughts. I used my binoculars to look out at the trees and the yards and the houses and the barns and the corn fields that I loved. I also used my binoculars to look at the moon. I thought I could see it better from the pole house because I was eight feet closer to it.

Anytime my friends came over, I always invited them to climb the chain ladder so I could show off the pole house that I was so proud of. One time, on a hot summer night, Mike Hobart and I laid our sleeping bags on the pole house floor and had a pole house sleepover. It wasn't very soft, but it was a fun adventure.

When the floor got dirty, I told my sister, Laura, to bring her little toy broom, and we could play *Little House on the Prairie*. She put on her bonnet and apron and then asked me to put up the real ladder for her. It was a small price to pay for a free cleaning service.

The next summer, I was riding my bike around Swygert, and I was shocked to see a pole house being constructed in the Hobart's side yard. It hurt my feelings. I thought they had stolen our idea. It wasn't nearly as tall as my pole house, but it did have real walls and a flat roof. It even had a window with real glass. After I got over being miffed, I went and had a closer look. Mike gave me a little tour. I told him it was nice, but I refused to be impressed. After the tour was over, I took another look at the Hobart's pole house from the ground level. I noticed a problem that gave me great satisfaction. I didn't say anything to Mike about it, but I could see with my naked eye that it wasn't plumb.

Making Tracks on the Tracks

When I was young, a freight train passed through Swygert exactly twice a day. In the morning, the train went from left to right. In the afternoon, it went from right to left; unless I was visiting my friend on the other side of the tracks, and then it was vice versa.

The dogs in Swygert knew when a train was approaching before the people did. They began to whine and pace back and forth when their keen ears detected the distant rumblings. When the train got near enough, the engineer would blow the horn to warn away any cars traveling on the Swygert blacktop. The train horn was extremely loud and very impressive. It was so loud that you could actually feel it. Every time the engineer sent out a blast, it hit me in the chest, and I could feel my sternum rattling.

When the horn blew, all the dogs in Swygert went completely nuts. They would close their eyes and lift their snouts in the air. They would each howl a long and mournful note. My mom said they howled because the horn hurt their ears; but I think it was more like a natural instinct. I think the train horn aroused the ancient wolf-part of their doggy brain.

It reminded them of some lost wolf howling in the distance. I think the dogs were actually howling back at the train in order to help it find its way back to the pack.

With the dogs howling and the train blowing its horn and the train engine rumbling and the steel wheels clicking along the track, it was completely impossible to hold a conversation. All normal Swygert life would come to a halt. It was like pushing the pause button on life. Adults would stop talking. Kids would stop playing. The elevator man would stop gossiping with the farmers. Anyone who was outdoors would look toward the tracks and watch the train go by. The engineer would wave, and we'd all wave back.

Then the all-important *count* would begin. For some reason, it was vitally important to know how long the train was. Every kid in Swygert, and some of the adults, would count each train-car as it passed by. You could see people all over Swygert standing in their yards mouthing the words: "fifty-one, fifty-two, fifty-three." Then finally, the red caboose would come at the end. There was usually another guy in the caboose to wave at. The noise of the clacking wheels would slowly subside. The dogs would calm down, and then some kid would yell out, "Sixty-Three-eee!" Then some other kid would dispute him, indignantly. "No, it was sixty-four! Did you count the engine? You have to count the engine!" "I did count the engine! It was sixty-three!" "No it was sixty-four! You messed up somewhere."

There were two sets of train tracks that ran through Swygert. They intersected the Swygert blacktop road about thirty feet apart from each other. Each time a car or truck passed by, there was a familiar "Kablunk, Kablunk" sound as the vehicle rolled over the two sets of tracks. I could tell the speed of each car from that sound. Cars traveling slowly went, "Kablunk ... ... Kablunk." Faster cars went, "Kablunk ... Kablunk," and on Saturday nights, when the race fans were on their way to the Fairbury stock-car races, it was more like, "Kablunkablunk."

Of the two sets of train tracks, one had shiny rails, and the other didn't. One rested on sturdy-looking, creosote-soaked railroad ties, and the other rested on cracked and rotten lumber. One had very little vegetation growing between the rails, and the other was chocked full of weeds. One had bright white limestone rocks between the ties, and the other had dusty pebbles. The shiny set of tracks was the main line, which the train traveled on twice a day. The other set was a sidetrack, and it was used only on rare occasions.

The kids in Swygert enjoyed messin' around on the railroad property. There were lots of interesting things to see and do. I don't remember any parents being overly worried about our safety, other than the usual, "You be careful over there." My dad said the train horn was so loud that it could blow small children out of the way.

Sometimes Swygert parents also enjoyed walks along the railroad. It was a poor man's nature trail. Trees grew all along the sides of the tracks, and there were plenty of birds to look at. The railroad was a good place to just walk and think and enjoy the great outdoors. Not to mention that wild asparagus grew along the tracks, and free food was a treasure for depression-born moms and dads.

My sister Jeny was a searcher, and she used the railroad tracks to search for things. When she wasn't searching for four-leaf clovers in our yard, then she was searching for Indian beads at the railroad. She somehow got the idea that Indians had dropped their beads along the railroad tracks, and with enough searching, she could find them lying in amongst the rocks and pebbles. She spent hours crouched down between the rails poking through the rocks. Every once in a while, she'd find a rock with a hole in it to prove that her endeavor was not in vain. Over the years, she amassed several of these Indian beads, and she kept them in a little glass bottle on her bedroom nightstand.

The Swygert kids liked to walk on the actual rails with one foot in front of the other like a gymnast on a balance beam. It was challenging, but with a little practice, most of the kids could manage to walk a long way without falling off. I remember walking on the rail down to the point where the sidetrack diverged from the main line. After some investigation, I figured out how the railroad men could cause one or more of the cars to leave the main line and roll onto the sidetrack. There was a mechanism with a big handle that was used to make it happen. The railroad men were smart enough to put a padlock on the mechanism to prevent any devilish temptation.

On rare occasions, the train would stop and leave a few hopper-cars on the sidetrack in order to be filled with grain at the elevator. I remember watching this process with fascination. The train would come to a stop and a man would get out and work the sidetrack mechanism. The train would proceed onto the sidetrack, and then it would come to another stop completely blocking any traffic traveling on the Swygert blacktop. The caboose man would unhitch the cars that were chosen to stay behind. As the train pulled away, there was a tremendous hissing sound when one car separated from another. My dad said it was the air-brakes. I never quite understood that. I thought an airplane should have air-brakes and a train should have train-brakes.

I remember one occasion when train-cars were left overnight on the sidetrack. The temptation for the kids of Swygert was overwhelming. We held our curiosity in check until after the elevator man had gone home, and then we nonchalantly ambled over toward the train-cars, hoping that no parents would take notice. We learned that it was never a good idea to ask permission for anything. That way we could always use the excuse, "You never told us not to."

One by one we approached the train-cars on the sidetrack. From up-close, those cars looked incredibly tall, and the steel wheels were almost as tall as I was. There was a lot of grease and grime on the ends of the axles. There were some huge springs down in the undercarriage. The couplers at the front and rear of each car looked like a giant, half-closed, human fist, just waiting for another giant hand to latch into it. I also saw the air-brake hose that my dad was talking about. It was dangling down at the rear of the last car. That hose was as thick as my arm.

When John Hobart arrived, he climbed right up on the crude metal ladder that was built on the side of each hopper-car. We all got a little braver when John was around. We followed him up the ladder one by one. The first step was a long way off the ground. When we got to the top, we could peer down into the empty hopper-car. It was humongous! We could see the mechanism in the bottom of the car used to empty the grain, and we could see remnants of corn kernels and soybeans down in the crevasses. The dregs of the left over grain had blue mold growing on it, and there was a faint smell of rotting vegetation.

One of the other boys started horsing around and pretended to push me in. For a split second I had quite a fright, but I held on tight to the sides of the car and indignantly yelled something like, "*HEYYYY!*" After we all had a good look down into the hopper-car, we climbed back down the ladder. Some kid picked up a handful of rocks and threw them up into the air. The rocks came down inside the hopper-car and made a tremendous clattering noise. Everybody instinctively ducted down into the weeds and sheepishly looked toward home in hopes that the noise didn't bring any parents to the window. The kid who threw the rocks received admonishment from the others. "What are you trying to do, get us in trouble?!"

One day, my friends, Myron Burton and Mike Hobart, asked me if I wanted to walk down to the trestle with them. I didn't know what a trestle was. They told me it was a bridge where the train crossed a little creek about two miles down the tracks, and we'd be gone for a few hours. My mom said it was OK, and told us to watch out for trains, and then she sent us on our trip with a thermos of water. (My mom never wanted anyone to be thirsty.)

This was a grand adventure for me. Mike and Myron had been there before, but it was my first time going on such a long hike down the tracks. We began our trip walking between the two rails of the main line, each of us looking at the ground to be sure of our footing. It was easy to trip on a railroad tie if you weren't careful. Soon, we passed by the Swygert Cemetery. The railroad track went right past it. It looked peaceful and serene with all of the headstones baking in the afternoon sun and the flowers and trees swaying slightly with the gentle breezes.

Myron pointed out a little place beside the tracks where his Mom liked to find asparagus. Mike was a little miffed and said, "How did you know about that place? That's where we go." Myron said, "No wonder it was all picked over the last time we came down here." We walked on in silence for a while until the little tiff blew over.

Next, we came upon the place where the high tension electric lines crossed over the train tracks. I could hear a buzzing sound as the electric current was coursing through the thick cables high overhead. The high tension lines didn't rest on any ordinary electric poles. They were draped over giant four-legged metal towers hundreds of feet in the air. As we passed under the wires, I looked out over the cornfields. I could see the path of the high tension lines traveling diagonally across the state of Illinois. The electric wires passed straight over any road, river, or farm, without so much as a how-do-you-do. The giant towers trespassed wherever they needed to go on a course that was unaltered by any obstacle.

As we walked on, we came upon a male red-winged blackbird that was very upset with us. He flew close over our heads and was squawking loudly. It's common for these birds to vigorously defend their nest, and I assumed that the nest must be nearby. Mike picked up a handful of rocks and heaved them at the bird yelling, "Get out-a-here!" The rocks missed, but the bird began to calm down as we continued to walk out of the vicinity.

Next we came to a place where the railroad crossed a gravel country road. Myron said, "We just walked a mile." I recognized the gravel road. It was one of the roads that our school bus traveled every day. School buses are required to stop at every railroad track, and I was quite familiar with this intersection where the bus driver stopped to check for trains. The intersection looked different from our vantage point, but we continued right on across the road and kept walking down the tracks.

Soon we came to a place where there were lots of trees on either side of the railroad. It reminded me of a green tunnel. I could hear birds chattering and bugs buzzing. The air was hot and steamy. The smell of summer was all around. I could see milkweeds, cockleburs, and cattails in the ditch on either side of the track. I started to get a lonely feeling like we were the only humans in the area. That heightened my sense of adventure. It was a rustically beautiful place with the trees in the height of their summer greenery. I envied the train engineer who must have enjoyed passing through places like that twice a day.

We walked on and on. The time passed very quickly for me with all of the new sites and sounds and smells. I listened to Mike and Myron chatting about one thing or another, but I generally just kept quiet and enjoyed the walk. We came to a place where the trees thinned out, and I could see a little waterway up ahead. Myron said, "We're almost there." As we got closer, I started to see the goal of our hike. The train track crossed the stream on a bridge that was supported by several big poles driven into the creek bed. The land under the train track fell away as we got closer. I could see that the train track ran about twenty feet above the creek.

When we reached the actual trestle, we had to be a little careful because they don't build railings for a train. It was strange to look down and see daylight between the railroad ties. I stepped cautiously to make sure that I wasn't putting my foot on an empty place. We all realized the danger and there was no horsing around. When we got to the other side, I followed Mike and Myron as they left the train track and walked down a slope through the weeds toward the creek. It was a bit muddy. I made a conscious effort not to complain. I didn't want the guys to think that I cared about getting a little mud on my shoes.

When we got down to the level of the creek, I looked up at the train track. It crossed high overhead. I was impressed by the size of the thick poles that supported the entire trestle structure. I remember thinking that it must have been a lot of work to build this bridge just so the train could cross a little creek.

I started to wonder what we'd do now that we had reached our goal. Myron sat down on a boulder and opened the lid of the thermos that my mom had sent with us. He took a swig and said, "You got good water at your house." (There was no city water in Swygert. Each family had its own well. Some wells tasted better than others.) Mike took a swig from the thermos and handed it to me. The thought crossed my mind to wipe off the spout, but I decided against it. I put the thermos straight up to my lips and drank. I didn't want the guys to think that I cared about germs and such.

Mike sat down on a rock and said, "Aw, this is the life." Myron found some bugs to look at. He showed me a red bug that was resting on a milkweed. He said it was a milkweed bug. He told me the bug would eventually turn into a monarch butterfly. I had no reason to doubt him, but it was hard to imagine. It didn't look anything like a butterfly at all. We all took our shoes off and waded in the creek. The mud at the bottom squished between my toes. I also stepped on a few unseen sharp rocks down there, but I didn't say anything about it. I wanted to act tough around the guys.

I poked around on the shore and found some little flat rocks. My father had previously taught me how to skip rocks, and I wanted to show off my talent. I held my arm close to the water and threw the rock with a sidearm motion the way my dad did it. My rock skipped nicely across the water, and I counted the skips in my head: one, two, three, four, five. I was hoping to impress the other guys with my ability. They looked unimpressed. I guess they already knew that trick. Mike picked up a flat rock with the intention of skipping it, but it was too heavy. His rock just plunked straight into the water. Myron scoffed and said, "Smooth move, Ex-lax." Then Myron gave it a try and had better luck. We all spent the next ten or fifteen minutes trying to see who could make the most skips until we had depleted the shore of all flat rocks. After we had our fill of skipping rocks and wading in the water and sitting around on the shore and looking at milkweed bugs, one of the guys thought it was time to head back, so we put our shoes back on and headed for home. It was a great trip. A good time was had by all.

The return trip seemed to go much faster. When we were nearly back home again, Mike stopped and crouched down near the rail. He wanted to show something to Myron and me. He told us that he had put a penny on the rail a few days prior, and he forgot about it. After a little bit of searching, he found a flat piece of brown metal in the rocks beside the rail. He said, "Here it is." It didn't look like a penny anymore. When I looked closely, I could barely make out Abe Lincoln's head, and it was all squashed out. Then I realized the train had run over Mike's penny, and this oblong, paper-thin, copper-colored thing was the result. I thought it was the coolest thing in the world. I went right home and asked my mom for a penny.

The Art of Bicycle Maintenance

When I was young, my bicycle was my most prized possession. I couldn't function without it. Hardly a summer day would go by when I didn't spend some time on my bike. It was my favorite thing to do. I never went anywhere in the neighborhood without riding my bike, and all of my friends did the same. Why walk when you can ride? Even when we weren't going anywhere in particular, we'd just ride up and down the road for fun. Sometimes we'd challenge each other to ride with no hands, and you weren't cool unless you knew how to pop a wheelie. The Swygert blacktop road was sparsely traveled so it made a good smooth place to ride. We also rode on the gravel cemetery road. It was bumpy, but it was great for making long dusty skid marks.

Back then, all of the bikes had coaster brakes rather than hand brakes. Those coaster brakes were terrific for making skid marks. My friends and I would have contests to see who could make the longest one. We'd ride a short distance down the road to get a good run at it, and then we'd turn around and pedal as fast as we could toward the designated skidding zone. After years of practice, I perfected my skidding technique. When I was at top speed, I'd stop peddling and coast for a second.

That gave me a little time to situate my left foot at the perfect three o'clock position for maximum braking torque. Then I'd stomp down on the pedal in the reverse direction, my rear tire would lock up, and the end result would be a long and lovely skid mark. Some kids liked to turn the front wheel back and forth while skidding in order to make a curvy skid mark, but I always went for substance over style. If you wanted to set the world record for longest skid mark, it was best to always skid in a straight line.

One year, my bike started misbehaving. The pedals wouldn't turn smoothly. I dreaded telling my dad about the problem, but my bike was vital to me, and I couldn't function without it. I finally screwed up my courage to let my dad know. I was expecting him to tell me I was "too hard on it," but I must have caught him on a good day. He said, "Lets take it down to the basement and have a look." That sounded great to me. I was always eager to work with my dad down in the basement.

We had a big basement that ran under the entire span of the house. It was an unfinished basement with a cement floor and walls made out of concrete block. There were a few basement windows up near the ground level and lots of exposed pipes and ducts and plenty of spider webs. The basement was always cool and damp even in the summer months. There was something about the dampness that gave the basement a wonderful musty smell. I loved the smell of the basement when I was a kid, and I still make it a point to go down there and have a good sniff when I go home to visit.

In my family, the basement was a man's domain. My sisters rarely ventured down there. I think the spiders kept them away.

My dad used the basement as his workshop. He had a table saw and a workbench and a grinding wheel and a lot of other tools down there. It made me feel manly to spend time with my dad down in the manly zone. Sometimes he let me help when he was working on one thing or another, but I never dared to touch anything unless he asked me to. My dad was moody and quick to anger. I learned that it was best just to watch and stay out of his way and wait patiently until he actually indicated a need for help. He was a man of few words. He didn't so much ask me for help, but rather indicated his desires by pointing and grunting. Over the years, I got very good at deciphering his grunts. We often worked in the basement for hours without a single English word being uttered between us. On the rare occasions when my dad actually spoke using real words, it was usually limited to the following set of phrases.

"Oh crock."
"Dad rat it."
"Dog gone it."
"Well I swan."
"Cotton pickin' thing."
"It's si wickety."
"It's bass ackwards."
"It's catty waumpus."
"It's slicker that snot."
"It's rougher than a cob."
"It costs an arm and a leg."
"It's the whole ball of wax."
"It's smack dab in the middle."
"It's six a one half a doz another."
"It don't amount to a hill a beans."

"It's crooked-er than a dog's hind leg."

"It's always in the last place you look."

"It's hotter than who wouldn't have it."

"It couldn't be any worse if I planned it."

"It's better than a poke in the eye with a sharp stick."

"Is that right?"

"That's a hell of a note."

"That's a fur piece to go."

"That's no great shakes."

"That's a hard row to hoe."

"That don't cut no ice with me."

"How do you rate?"

"How do you manage?"

"Don't that frost ya?"

"Can you fathom that?"

"Do I hafta draw you a picture?"

"Are you nervous?"

"You're pullin' my leg."

"You're S-O-L."

"Keep your shirt on."

"Keep your pants on."

"Put your clod hoppers on."

"Don't fly off the handle."

"Quit your belly achin'."

"Quit runnin' off at the head."

"Who's makin' all that racket?"

"I'll skin you alive."

"You jabber box."

"You goof ball."

"You gum sucker."

"You make a better door than you do a window."

"Why do you always speak in riddles?"

"I think you talk just to hear your own head rattle."

"I think your eyes are bigger than your stomach."

"I'm a day late and a dollar short."

"I'm between a rock and a hard place."

"I put my pants on one leg at a time."

"Well kiss my foot."

"Well big hairy deal."

"Ain't no hairs on that."

"Ain't seen hide nor hair of it."

"There's more than *one* way to skin a cat."

"There's not enough room in here to sling a cat."

"The shortest distance between two points is a straight line."

"Well what's *that* got to do with the price of tea in China?"

After we carried my bike down to the basement, my dad started moving sawhorses around in order to make some room for us. Then he laid some newspapers down on the floor. I was getting impatient with all of this preliminary stuff. I wanted to dig into the problem and get down to work. Of coarse, I didn't say anything. I never knew what would set him off, so I just kept my mouth shut and tried to be patient. Finally, after a half hour of preparing our workspace, my dad finally got down to business. He turned my bike upside down on the floor. It was propped-up in a three-point stance with the handlebars and seat touching the floor and the wheels up in the air. It was a very convenient position for bicycle diagnosis.

My dad began to look things over in his slow and methodical way. He wiggled the chain and wiggled the spokes and wiggled the pedals and wiggled the fenders. He slowly cranked the crank around and around. I watched the rear wheel turning.

Every time around, the crank would catch and hesitate at a certain spot. I got excited and said, "See, that's what I'm talking about!" He said, "Keep your shirt on, Shorty."

Dad kept cranking slowly around and around. He stared at the crank and stared at the chain. He turned slowly and then quickly. Each time around, the crank would catch again in that same place. He turned the crank backwards and stopped the rear wheel using the coaster brake. He took two hands and wiggled the crank in its pivot point. He said, "Lota slop in there." He started cranking the crank again: around and around. After ten minutes of this, I was about to burst with impatience. I wanted to fix it, not just stand around and look at it. I couldn't stand it anymore. I finally opened my mouth and said, "What's wrong with it, Dad?" He frowned and said in a sarcastic tone, "Howdya expect *me* to know everything?" I got the message. I sat on a sawhorse and let my legs dangle. I unconsciously started wiggling my right foot. Dad said, "Are you nervous?"

After some more pedaling and testing and grunting comments about one thing or another, my dad finally went over to the bench and grabbed his tool box and brought it back to our work area. He opened the toolbox and found an open-end 9/16th inch wrench. He used the wrench to remove the pedals from the crank. Dad used the same wrench to loosen up the rear wheel, and the chain became very slack. He then derailed the chain from the main sprocket and let it dangle. With the chain out of the way, I couldn't resist the temptation. I got up from the sawhorse, and I gave the crank a spin. I was amazed how easily it turned without the burden of the rear wheel, but I still could feel that catch. My dad said, "Keep your pants on, Shorty."

Next, my dad removed the top tray from his toolbox and started rummaging in the bottom where the bigger wrenches were. He picked up his very biggest crescent wrench. There was a sizable nut where the pedal crank was attached to the frame. My dad started turning that big nut *clockwise* with the crescent wrench, and it became loser and loser. My dad said, "See that ... left-handed threads ... they do that so it won't come loose when you pedal." I never heard of left-handed threads, or right-handed threads for that matter. I must have given my dad a puzzled look, and he said in an annoyed tone of voice, "Do I hafta draw you a picture? Look which way I'm turning it. ... You see that? ... It's bass ackwards." My brain did a little search, and I found something in there about tightening things clockwise and loosening them counterclockwise, and then I finally understood what he was talking about. I said, "Ohhhhh," and my dad mocked me in a sarcastic voice saying, "Ohhhhh ... well I'll be dogged ... imagine that ... left-handed threads."

After the big nut came off, my dad managed to slip the crank completely out of its hole by snaking it this way and that. He laid the crank on the newspaper, and I saw that it was attached to the main sprocket as a single unit. I was fascinated. It was the first time I ever saw a bicycle taken apart. The bicycle looked funny with no pedals and no sprocket. We were left with a big hole in the bike frame where the crank used to be. The hole was full of grease. My dad plunged his fingers into all that grease and started feeling around. He found something, pulled it out, and showed it to me. He said, "Well *that's* a hell of a note." It was a little metal ball about the size of a pea. He said, "Bearings fell apart." I didn't know what a bearing was, but I didn't dare to ask. I took his word for it, and I had no doubt that it was indeed "a hell of a note."

My dad kept fishing around in the hole. He pulled out more greasy metal balls and also a thing that looked like a little metal donut ring. The donut had a few of the little metal balls inside it, but I could also see that several were missing. My dad told me this donut shaped thing was called a "bearing race," and it was "all shot." He pulled another bearing race out from the other side, and it was "all shot" too.

This was all new territory for me. I was learning new things that I had never seen before; but the most important thing I learned was that mechanical things could be understood, and problems could be diagnosed by using some common tools and a lot of good observation. I had the feeling that I could have done this work myself if I had taken a notion to do it. After this day, I'd be much braver about tackling repair jobs on my own. I watched how my dad tackled the job, slowly, one step at a time, with lots of patience and observation. He took his time and figured things out as he went along. It was an important life lesson for me, and I'd use it over and over again throughout the rest of my life.

My dad told me to get some paper towels, and then he proceeded to clean all of the old grease off the crank and out of the big hole in the bike frame. He even cleaned the broken bearing races. When most of the black grease was cleaned up, my dad took a fresh paper towel and dipped it into a little bit of gasoline, then he used that gassy paper towel to do the final clean up. After another excruciating half hour, watching my dad meticulously clean everything off, he finally said, "I don't know about you, but I'm hungry."

After lunch, we both hopped in his old white Buick. I didn't know where we were going, and I certainly didn't dare to ask. I hoped it had something to do with the bike repair. My dad turned on WBBM News Radio Seventy-Eight, and he pushed in the knob of the cigarette lighter. A half-mile down the road, the cigarette lighter made its familiar click, and the knob popped up to indicate that it was ready for use. Dad pulled it out of its hole, and I saw the bright red glow as he used it to light up a King Edward cigar. After fifteen minutes of driving, I recognized we were in Fairbury. We parked in front of the Coast to Coast hardware store. I hadn't said a single word all the way to Fairbury. My dad turned off the engine and said sarcastically, "You sure are gabby today."

I followed Dad into the store. After passing a few aisles, we came to the bicycle section. I saw bike-tires and inner-tubes and reflectors and peddles and bicycle-seats. Without thinking, I stood right in front of my father, and he said, "You make a better door than you do a window." After I moved out of the way, he started looking at some small metal parts. He picked up two of those bearing races. I was completely amazed. I couldn't believe you could actually buy something like that in a store. I never heard of a bearing race in my life, and here they were, waiting for us to buy them. At that moment, I felt like the Coast to Coast was my best friend in the world. Dad had brought along one of the broken bearing races for comparison purposes. He held up a new one beside the old one to check for size. It looked like a match to me, and my dad confirmed it. He said, "Looks like six a one half a doz another." (I was convinced that my father spoke his own strange dialect of the English language.) Along with the two new bearing races, my dad also bought me a new front tire. He said, "That one you have now is slicker than snot."

After we got the things we needed at the hardware store, we both *got our ears lowered* at the barbershop in Fairbury. In my family, it was a sin to make a special trip into town for just one thing, so we always tried to get several things accomplished. Nobody needed an appointment to get a haircut in those days. You just walked in and waited your turn. My dad liked the little barbershop in Fairbury. It was run by a friendly, stoop-shouldered guy who had worn a hole in the linoleum after standing in the same spot for thirty years. While we waited for our turn, I watched the red and white striped barber pole spinning outside the window. The red stripe was painted in a spiral. My eyes followed the spiral red line as it wound its way up to the top. I noticed that no matter what part of the stripe I looked at, my eyes would eventually end up at the top. That fascinated me. It reminded me of an auger. My eyes acted as the payload being pushed along from the bottom to the top. I tried it again, and the same thing happened. I held up my finger as a reference point to follow the red stripe, and my finger ended up at the top of the pole too. My dad looked up from the dog eared, two year old, *Popular Science* magazine that he was reading, gave me a half smile, and said, "You goof ball."

When we got back home, we started putting my bike back together. Before we could put in the new bearing races, we had to pack them with grease. My dad showed me how to force grease into the bearing race so that every crack and crevasse was filled all around the little ball bearings. After showing me how, he let me pack the second one. I took two fingers full of grease from the grease gun and began to force the grease in around the ball bearings. I was not nearly as deft at the work, but my dad allowed me to struggle and complete the job on my own. He said, "Take your time and do it right, son." When I finally finished, I had grease clear up to my elbows. My dad said, "Well I swan. How do you manage?" Then he proceeded to clean *me* up with a paper towel dampened with gasoline. (Gas was my dad's favorite cleaning agent.)

Of course, I thought my bike would be fixed in one afternoon, but my dad was a very slow and methodical worker. He never took a shortcut. It ended up taking two or three days to finish the job. After fixing the bearings, we changed the front tire and that took one whole evening. Then my dad proceeded to tear apart the rear axle. He wanted to check the coaster brake and the bearings in the rear. We didn't need any new parts for the rear axle, but we spent another lovely hour or two cleaning out old grease and packing in new grease. I also remember that my dad decided to soak the bicycle chain in a coffee can full of gas. The next day my chain looked much cleaner, and then we proceeded to meticulously oil every little chain link, one by one, with a drop of Three-In-One Oil.

When the job was finally complete, we took the bike outside. Dad told me to test it out. I rode around the driveway, and the pedals worked great. I didn't feel the catch anymore. I said, "It works good now," but my dad wasn't satisfied. He told me to keep riding in a circle. As I rode, he watched the wheels turning and watched the crank cranking. He called me back and then used his fingers to test the amount of slack in the chain. He looked closely at the back tire and asked me, "Don't you hear that fender rubbing?" We spent another half hour using wrenches in the driveway to make all of the final fender adjustments.

After Dad put his tools away and walked into the house, I rode all around the neighborhood. My bike was working great, and I wanted to show off my new front tire. It had a red stripe all around the sidewall. I told all my friends that we had *overhauled* my bike. I threw around my new words and tried to impress them. "The bearings were all shot," I said.

I felt a little superior with my new knowledge of bearings and sprockets and left-handed threads. I felt like I could fix anything just by following my dad's slow methodical methods. I started looking for things to fix. My poor little sister, Laura, couldn't ride her bike in peace without me coming toward her with a 9/16ths wrench in my hand saying, "Don't you hear that fender rubbing?"

The Machine

~~~~~~

For several years there was an extra riding lawn mower that sat in the front of our garage. My dad bought it at an auction sale, but we never actually used it to mow the lawn. I'm sure he had some vague plans for it, but the old Yardman mower was still going strong, so there was no compelling reason to put the extra one into service. The Great Depression taught my parents to keep everything, because "you might need that someday."

Once, when I was messin' around in the garage, the unused mower caught my attention. I had seen it sitting there many times before, but for some reason, this time, I got an urge to investigate. Perhaps there was some serendipitous convergence of my age and my experience that culminated in a grand compulsion to explore the possibilities. (Either that, or I had nothing better to do.)

It was an odd-looking machine with large wheels in the front and small wheels in the back. The wheels were made of steel and were clad with a hard rubber tread. There were no tires to inflate. The steering wheel rested horizontally atop a shaft that jutted straight up in front of the drivers seat. The cutting blades were not located under the belly, like most riding mowers, but were attached to a blade deck which was supposed to hang, cantilever style, on the front of the mower. The odd looks of the mower and its strange wheels reminded me of a military vehicle. I imagined that it could travel over rough terrain like an army jeep.

Other than a lot of dust and cobwebs, the mower wasn't in terrible shape. I didn't see any missing parts. Although I knew it hadn't been started in several years, ideas began to develop in my head. I wondered if I could start the engine. I wondered if I could teach myself to drive it. I wondered how fast it would go. I wondered if it would climb hills and cross ditches as suggested by its rugged appearance.

Since no one had used it for several years, I had the feeling that maybe the statute of limitations had run out. I got an idea that the unused mower was up for grabs. If no one else wanted it, then maybe I could adopt it as my own. Whenever there was any doubt in a situation like that, I opted not to ask permission. It was never a good idea to give your parents a chance to say no.

It didn't take long for me to push the mower out of the garage and into the light of day. I left the blade deck in the garage because I didn't intend to mow with it. My first task was to check the oil, gas, and air filter. I was happy to see that it had a Briggs and Stratton Engine. I was familiar with those. I verified that the air filter was clean, and then I filled the necessary liquids.

I located the engine control lever and moved it to the choke position. I got a tingling feeling in my stomach as I was preparing for my first attempt at starting the engine. The starter rope had a big substantial rubber handle that fit well into my hands. I slowly pulled the rope about six inches to get the slack out and stopped at the point where I could feel the resistance of the engine. I spread my feet apart and hunkered down a little in preparation for making the two handed quick and deliberate motion that I had seen my dad use on the Yardman mower so many times before. I closed my eyes and engaged my muscles and gave the rope an almighty tug. There was a lot of resistance, but I was able to pull the rope, and I heard the familiar glug, glug, glug, that indicated the engine was turning. It didn't start, but that didn't surprise me. I really hadn't expected it to start on the first pull, but I was glad to know the engine wasn't seized up inside.

After ten or twelve more pulls, my spirits began to fall. The engine hadn't given me any indication that it wanted to run. I hadn't heard any encouraging sounds other than the same glug, glug, glug, each time. I stopped to rest my arms and catch my breath. My mind started running through what little engine diagnostic information I had stored in there. Then I noticed something. I saw a wire dangling down near the spark plug. The wire had a metal connector on the end, and I knew it was supposed to be connected to the spark plug. I easily snapped it back on. I wondered if my dad had purposely disconnected the spark plug wire for storage.

After two or three more pulls, the engine coughed and sputtered a little. My stomach started to tingle like crazy. It was a very encouraging and familiar sound. I knew what to do next. I slid the engine control lever away from the choke position and onto the full throttle position. I mentally crossed my fingers and gave the rope one more solid tug. The engine fired a few times and then revved up to a steady speed. I could hear that it was running smoothly. I was amazed. It sounded great. It sounded exactly like a one-cylinder, three and a half horsepower Briggs and Stratton engine was supposed to sound. I was overjoyed and proud of myself. It felt good to know that I had the knowledge to bring a neglected engine back to life.

With the engine running, I sat down on the seat and proceeded to teach myself how to drive the odd looking machine. I looked down between my legs at the two levers that where there. One was marked "R N 1 2 3." The other was not marked at all. I depressed the foot pedal, slid the marked lever to the "1" position and then slowly released the pedal. It was a little scary not knowing exactly what was going to happen, but I had driven other riding lawn mowers before, and I assumed it would go forward slowly in first gear. I was right. The mower began to move forward! I began to drive around the yard and quickly became confident in how to go, stop, and turn. I tried all of the gears and was glad to see that they all worked: even reverse.

After a few minutes of driving, I realized that the mower wasn't a speed demon even in third gear, but I began to understand why it looked so strange. For every car, truck, tractor, bicycle, motorcycle, and lawn mower that I had ever seen in my life, the front wheels were responsible for making turns. That was not the case for this strange machine. The large wheels in the front faced forward at all times. They had no ability to turn. When I used the steering wheel, it was actually the rear wheels that responded. As my dad would say, it was bass ackwards.

I found by experimentation that rear wheel steering was a wonderful thing. It allowed the mower to make very sharp turns. I began driving around the backyard making quick, ninety-degree turns to the left and right. I had heard the older boys talk about making *donuts,* and I decided to see what kind of donuts my new machine could make. I put the mower in high gear with the engine at full throttle. I cruised down the gravel cemetery road, and then I suddenly cranked the steering wheel to the left as far as it would go. The mower responded immediately and began turning in a tight circle right in the middle of the road. It felt like a carnival ride, and I was spinning like a top. After four or five revolutions, I straightened out the wheel and then stopped to inspect the results. There was a circular mark in the road where my wheels had been turning. I couldn't wait to show off my donut the next time I saw my friends.

After the first day, I adopted the odd looking little lawn mower as my own. I felt that it belonged to me because I had brought it back to life. My dad worked the second shift. It took several days for our schedules to coincide enough for him to notice me driving the mower around. I don't remember any strong objections, but he wasn't as impressed as I thought he might be. I told him that I fixed the engine. I told him the spark plug wire was loose. He said, "Well big hairy deal."

I began using the odd looking mower periodically as a recreational vehicle. What it lacked in speed, it made up for in agility. It was able to climb small hills and run over rough terrain, to say nothing about the sharp turns it could make. I drove around Swygert looking for ditches, hills, and tall weeds. The railroad property had an abundance of those. I found that the little mower could usually make it through just about anything, and if it couldn't, I'd just make a sharp turn and go around.

On the rare occasions when the mower got stuck, I discovered that I could get unstuck by pushing on the mysterious unmarked level down by my ankles. I was never quite sure of the real purpose for that lever, but I began calling it the *positraction knob*. I once heard John Hobart telling someone that his car had positraction. I liked to think that my mower had it too.

The Swygert neighborhood kids had seen me driving around in the odd looking mower, and they were mildly impressed. I told them about the spark plug wire. I pointed out the strange rear wheel steering. I told them that it had positraction and, "Man. It turns on a dime!" I sometimes let other kids drive it. We took turns plowing through the tall weeds on the railroad property. We started calling it *The Machine*, and it became a neighborhood hit.

The color of *The Machine* was brown. It was a perfectly acceptable color for a lawn mower, but for a fun recreational vehicle, it just wouldn't do. One day my friends and I decided to make a change. Using some spray paint and masking tape, we changed its color from brown to silver. We also added black racing stripes. Mike Hobart brought over a lawn mower seat that he found laying around at his place. The new seat bolted on surprisingly easily, just as if there were some kind of lawn mower seat interchangeability standard. We liked the new seat better because it had a backrest.

One time John Hobart asked me to let him drive *The Machine*. Of course, I couldn't refuse. John was four or five years older. It was an honor if John took an interest in anything that us little kids were doing. John hopped aboard, put it into third gear, and started rolling down the road. I saw him reach down near the side of the engine. The engine revved up much faster than normal and *The Machine* went faster than I had ever seen it go. (I'll bet it must have been going at least four miles per hour!) Mike and I chased after John on foot. When we caught up, I yelled over the roar of the engine, *"How'd you do that!"* He grinned and pointed to a little lever near the engine and yelled back, *"The governor!"* For two seconds, I had a vision of a guy in a business suit sitting behind a big desk up at the state capitol, but then I came back to reality. Must be a different kind of governor, I thought.

As soon as John gave me back *The Machine*, I hopped aboard and tried my luck with the governor. It didn't look like something you were supposed to mess with, but I gently pulled the little lever with my finger, and the engine began to roar. It sounded a bit out of control, and it worried me a little. I didn't have an owners manual, but I doubted very strongly if it would say, "If you need a little more speed, pull on the governor." I decided to use it sparingly, but it was a nice little trick to keep in my back pocket.

I think driving *The Machine* struck a chord in John's imagination. Swygert contained a feature that was perfect to help him incubate his plan. It was called Childers' Junkyard. Some guy, named Mr. Childers, bought a half-acre plot of land in Swygert, but instead of building a house on his land, he commenced filling his lot with all manner of wrecked cars, rusty old trucks, broken down tractors, and various other kinds of discarded vehicles and machines. When you live in the country, there are no rules.

One would think that Mr. Childers would have used his junkyard as a business to make money, but there was never any evidence of that. No business sign was ever erected. No customers ever came to buy anything. Mr. Childers never actually spent any time in his junkyard tending the business. He'd just show up three or four times a year to deposit some more junk. Over the years, the lot filled up with more and more stuff. Everything just sat there and rusted.

My parents strictly warned me to stay away from that dangerous place, but it was an overwhelming draw for the older kids in Swygert. How could any teenage boy possibly resist? There was no fence, there was never anyone there, and the whole place was full of old cars. That's heaven for teenage guys.

I sometimes saw John Hobart messin' around in the junkyard with his friends. They seemed never to tire of busting out the windows and headlights of the hulks that sat there silently rusting away, but one day they actually decided to do something constructive. After seeing me having so much fun with *The Machine*, they decided to build one of their own. John found some kind of vehicle skeleton in the junkyard. He decided to help himself to it. He coaxed his friends into helping him bring it back to life. It kept them occupied all summer.

The thing they found was even stranger looking than my machine. It was smaller than a car, but it seemed too big to be a lawn mower. It had four wheels, but there wasn't a body. It was just a frame with a steering wheel, a gearshift, and some sort of transmission. No one really knew what it was, but that didn't stop them from working on it. Using the ample supply of spare parts lying around the junkyard, they proceeded to fix the tires and bolt on a seat; then they equipped it with a ten horsepower lawnmower engine.

When I saw what they were building, I was a little put out. I thought they'd stolen my idea, but I soon got over it. I even helped them out one day when John came over asking to borrow some super-glue. He broke the valve stem off one of the tires, and he wanted to glue it back on. After several weeks, they actually got their machine working. It was much bigger than my machine, but it didn't go any faster.

We often drove our two machines together around the neighborhood. The railroad property provided some challenging terrain. There were ditches on either side of the railroad track that sometimes contained water. There were also plenty of tall weeds to plow through. We enjoyed driving our machines over, around, and through the obstacles, always on the lookout for a challenging hill or ditch to drive across.

When school started in the fall, it curtailed our R.V. activities, but we still did some driving after school and on weekends. One of our first art class assignments, that year, was to create a decorated T-shirt that we could wear after it was finished. I liked the idea. It gave me the opportunity to create a racing jersey to be worn while driving *The Machine*. The miserly principal of Owego School didn't like the idea. She thought it was too much to ask of the parents to supply a plain white T-shirt for art class, but the art teacher prevailed. We all showed up on art day with a T-shirt to use in our project.

The process we used to adorn our T-shirts was rather surprising to me. We used crayons to draw on our shirts, and then we made the drawing permanent by ironing the shirt with wax paper. We were told that this would make the crayon drawing permanent, so that our hard work wouldn't be washed down the drain.

I knew, right away, how I wanted my shirt to look. I wanted big numbers on the front and the back. I also wanted my last name on the back, so that it would look like a race driver's jersey. I started by putting a big number "64" on the front of the shirt. It was my favorite number at the time. After doing that, I was disappointed to find that I had accidentally placed the digits off center. The "64" was too far to the left. I covered up my mistake by adding a big zero so that my number became "640." I put a matching "640" on the back, along with my last name, then I took my shirt over to the ironing station and made my work permanent.

The very next Saturday, I proudly put on my new racing jersey and went straight out to drive *The Machine*. I planned to drive around the neighborhood in hopes that one of the kids would see me all duded up in my new racing jersey. Before starting the engine, I always checked the oil and gas as my dad had taught me. When I started the engine, it happily started on the first pull and ran smoothly like usual. My ears told me the engine was running fine, but my eyes saw that something was terribly wrong.

There were black globs of stuff spurting up from the engine. It went up high in the air and came back down like black rain. I was stunned for a second. The black stuff was hitting me in the face. It was landing in my hair. It was splashing all over the cement in front of the garage. After a few seconds of fear and panic, I was able to gather up my wits. I fought my way through the black rain and managed to find the throttle control. I slide it to the off position, and the engine came to a halt. I was relieved to see the black rain also subsided.

I was afraid to know what caused it. My worst fear was that the engine had blown up, and I wouldn't be able to ride *The Machine* anymore. I felt scared and confused and worried, and I was trembling all over. I reluctantly took a closer look at the engine, dreading to find a blown gasket or maybe a hole in the engine block. As I looked closer, I was relieved to see that the problem was something simple. I was so glad that it wasn't something serious, but I was mad at myself for being so stupid. When I checked the oil before starting the engine, I accidentally left the oil cap off. The black rain was engine oil, and it was propelled into the air by the engine. I thought I knew a lot about engines, but I never knew that would happen. I started cleaning up the mess when a terrible thought hit me. I slowly looked down at my brand new racing jersey. It was ruined.

America's Favorite Pass Time: TV

~~~~~~

When I was young, we had a big black and white TV. All of the shows were in shades of gray, and it looked just fine to me. Color TV wasn't common back then, and you don't miss what you never had. Our TV was called a console type. It looked like a piece of furniture with a genuine, imitation, wooden enclosure cabinet. The TV sat on the north wall in the front room.

Our TV had a big rotary knob that was used to change the channels. Nobody had a remote control in those days. If you wanted to change the channel you had to get up from your chair, walk to the TV, and turn the knob. When changing channels, the knob would go clunk ... clunk ... clunk. My parents insisted that we turn the knob slowly: one clunk at a time. We'd get in trouble if we clunked it too fast. My dad said it was hard on the TV.

There was no cable TV out in the country. We got our TV reception using a big antenna on the roof of the house. The antenna was pointed toward Chicago. We could get four channels and maybe five if the weather was just right. Channel 2 was CBS. Channel 5 was NBC. Channel 7 was ABC. Channel

9 was WGN. On clear days, we could sometimes also get channel 11. I didn't really care if channel 11 came in or not. It was a public television station. They only broadcast *Sesame Street*, *Mr. Rogers*, and *Zoom*. My little sister Laura watched *Zoom* once in a while, and she learned how to speak Ubbi-Dubbi language.

Sometimes we'd notice a fuzzy picture coming in on channel 3 as we slowly clunked by. My dad was always amazed when channel 3 would come in. He'd get excited and say, "Look at that! That's coming in off the back of the antenna all the way from Champaign, Illinois! Can you *fathom* that?" We couldn't tell the difference between the back of an antenna or the front, but we said, "Wow," and made other appropriate noises and pretended to *fathom* it.

Once in a while a storm or a strong wind would turn the antenna a little bit, and then the TV reception would be terrible. Every time that happened, my dad would have to get out the big extension ladder, climb up on the roof, and re-aim the antenna toward Chicago. He'd turn the antenna a little bit and holler down, "How's that look?" My mom would holler back out the window, "It's getting worse," or "It's getting better." My mom didn't have a very loud voice, so we'd station a kid or two out in the yard in order to relay the messages. "It's getting better." "*It's getting better!*" "A little more." "*A little more!*" "It's good now." "*It's good now!*" After that, my dad would use a wrench to tighten the antenna so it wouldn't happen again, but it always happened again. My dad would proclaim, "What we really need is a rotor and a deep fringe antenna with a signal booster." I'd agree with him, wholeheartedly, without having the foggiest idea what he was talking about.

My absolute favorite channel was WGN channel 9 from Chicago. It was an independent station not affiliated with any national network; therefore, they could afford the time to play all of the really good shows like *The Flintstones* and *Gilligan's Island*. In the summer, WGN televised each and every Chicago Cubs home game from the friendly confines of Wrigley Field. The announcer was Jack Brickhouse. He announced the games and also rooted for the Cubs right along with the rest of us. Each time the Cubs hit a homer, his trademark catchphrase was, "Hey-Hey!" Wrigley Field had no lights, so every home game was played in the lazy summer afternoons.

During the school year, my sisters and I watched channel 9 before school. The *Ray Raynor Show* was on from 7:00 AM to 8:00 AM. It was wonderful. Ray played a lot of *Bug's Bunny* cartoons. He also spent time showing all the kids how to build crafty little projects of one sort or another. Ray's projects never looked as good as the example projects built by some off-camera guy named Chauncey. Ray was always talking to Chauncey, but we never got to see what he looked like. Ray would say, "Am I doing this right Chauncey?" "What's next, Chauncey?" "Why doesn't mine look like yours, Chauncey?"

Sometimes Ray would put on a drum major jacket and march around the studio with his friend, Chelveston the duck. It was a real live duck named Chelveston. The duck would follow Ray around, and then he'd hop into his little tub of water, and Ray would feed him a head of lettuce. Chelveston loved lettuce. There would be lettuce flying all over the place.

I always liked the segment when Ray would tell jokes with his pal, Cuddly Dudley, a puppet dog with huge ears. He asked the viewers to send in their favorite jokes and riddles, then Ray would take a stroll over to Cuddly Dudley's doghouse, and they would both read the jokes on the air. I knew a girl who sent a joke to the Ray Raynor show. Her name was Susan Fraher. (It rhymes with fair.) Susan had a color TV at her house, and she wrote her joke on a piece of purple paper with a frayed edge. Every day, Susan would watch the Cuddly Dudley segment. She could actually see her purple piece of paper in the joke pile that Ray carried around. Each day her purple paper got closer and closer to the top of the pile. She anxiously watched, day after day, and she'd tell all the kids at school that her purple paper would soon be at the top of the pile. Finally, one day it happened. Ray Raynor actually said the words, "OK this joke was sent in from … ahhhh … Susan Fraw-here, all the way from … ahhhh … Pontiac, Illinois." Then Ray let Cuddly Dudley read the joke. When Susan got to school, all the kids were impressed because they heard Susan's name mentioned on TV. For the next three or four weeks, all the kids would say, "Hello Susan Fraw-here," imitating the way that Ray Raynor had mispronounced it.

After the *Ray Raynor Show*, we still had about twenty minutes to watch *The Garfield Goose Show* before the bus came to pick us up. The host of the show was Frazier Thomas. He always wore an official looking military type coat with fringe on each shoulder. He basically spent the show talking to two speechless hand puppets that only Mr. Thomas could understand: Garfield Goose and Romberg Rabbit. Garfield Goose wore a crown on his head and when he talked, he clapped the two halves of his beak together. It sounded like someone tapping out Morse code as his beak went clack, clack,

clack. Frazier Thomas could understand him perfectly, and he'd interpret everything Garfield said for the benefit of the audience. Romberg Rabbit spent all his time whispering things in Frazier's ear, and then Mr. Thomas would once again relay all the important things that Romberg had to say.

Each day, Frazier Thomas played a new episode of a serial cartoon known as, *The Adventures of Clutch Cargo with his pals Spinner and Paddlefoot.* It was a strange, cheaply made, cartoon. All of the characters were stationary. The only things that moved were their lips. We didn't mind. If Frazier Thomas thought it was good, then we thought it was good. It was fun to follow the continuing adventures as Clutch Cargo, Spinner, and Paddlefoot got themselves into and out of dangerous situations.

Another segment on *The Garfield Goose Show* was called, *The Funny Company.* It was an educational cartoon in which the characters invited the audience to enter the Funny Company Clubhouse and learn about new things each day. I will never forget the theme song.

> We have a company,
> That you can join for free,
> And kids in every neighborhood belong.
> It's the Funny Company,
> Cause it's just for fun you see,
> So, come a running when you hear our song.
> Come to order, Come to order,
> Says our President,
> And when the Funny Company meets,
> You get what he presents.
> Things to see and things to do,

Stories, Songs, Toys.
All sorts of things of interest,
And fun for girls and boys.
BAAAAAAAAP.

That last BAAAAAP was an Indian named Super Chief.
He didn't talk. He just opened his mouth and said BAAAAP
like a train horn.

Saturday morning TV was heaven for kids. Cartoons were
on every channel from 7:00 AM to noon. As soon as we opened
our eyes, we'd pop out of bed and go straight to the TV. We'd
sit on the floor in the front room all morning, with our pajamas
on, watching cartoons. Laura and I allowed Jeny to make all the
decisions about which shows to watch. We assumed she knew
what the cool shows were. We watched *The Groovie Ghoulies*,
The Archie Show, *The Banana Splits*, *Josie and the Pussycats*, *H.
R. Pufnstuf*, and *Fat Albert*. We also liked *The Wacky Races* with
Penelope Pitstop, Dick Dastardly, and his dog, Muttley.

Breakfast cereal was heavily advertised on Saturday
mornings. I'm sure my mom appreciated those TV networks
filling out minds with Frankenberry, Count Chocula, Cocoa
Puffs, Lucky Charms, Kix, Trix, Cap'n Crunch, and Froot
Loops. I remember a big advertising campaign in which there
was a contest to decide which cereal the kids of America liked
better: Quisp or Quake. (Actually, it was the same stuff just
shaped differently.) Quisp was some sort of little flying character
with a propeller on his head, and the cereal was shaped like little
saucers. Quake was a big guy that caused the earth to quake
when he walked, and his cereal was shaped like a jagged yellow
Cheerio. There were several different Quisp and Quake TV

commercials. They asked all the kids to write in and vote for their favorite. Jeny was a big Quisp supporter, and she actually joined the Quisp fan club. I always thought that Quisp was a feminine looking character, so I chose to support Quake. Jeny started throwing insults at my candidate. She said Quake was a big, dumb, doofus, and she wouldn't dream of even touching the box of Quake cereal that Mom bought for me. I threw back insults towards her Quisp candidate, but I generally resorted to the old standard comeback, "Oh Yeah?" I was very disappointed when, after several months, Quisp won the popularity contest. I think they actually stopped making Quake cereal after that.

The cereal companies were quite inventive. They tried anything to get kids to ask their mom's for one kind or another. Putting a prize in the box was quite common. I know that trick suckered me in several times. At the grocery store, Mom would ask me, "Will you really eat that stuff, or do you just want it for the prize?" I would plead, "No, really Mom. It looks good. I think I'll like it." Actually, I was not a picky eater. I could eat any cereal if it had a prize inside, except for Raisin Bran. (Yuck.)

I remember one really cool cereal advertising trick. Jeny was a big fan of the Saturday morning cartoon called *The Archie Show.* The characters in the show started their own garage band called *The Archie's.* One of their songs, *Sugar, Sugar,* actually became a hit and was played on pop radio stations. The cereal company that advertised on *The Archie Show* somehow figured out a way to press a 45 RPM record right into the cardboard on the back of the cereal box. Jeny carefully cut out the record on the specified dotted lines. When we played it on our record player, it actually sounded halfway decent: not bad for a cardboard record.

There was another popular character on TV commercials called Frito Bandito. He advertised Frito's corn chips. Jeny really liked this little guy, and she began collecting Frito Bandito stuff. She had a Frito Bandito pencil eraser and no one was allowed to use it.

When my dad woke up on Saturday mornings, he liked to watch *Johnny Quest*. Johnny roamed the world with his father and another guy named Race Bannon getting into one adventure after another. Johnny had a friend named Hadji and a dog named Bandit who also went along and got into a bunch of trouble.

When my sister Joyce finally emerged from bed, we watched *The Monkees* with her. It wasn't a cartoon. It was a bizarre show with four goofy guys doing weird stuff and saying strange things. One of them was never seen without a blue stocking cap on his head. He even wore it when he was swimming. The four goofy guys were in a rock band together, and they actually had several hit songs. Joyce had a couple of 45 RPM records by *The Monkees*. Her friend, Carol, would come over to our house once in a while and listen to records with Joyce.

The Monkees was over at noon. Noon was the end of the line for the kid shows on Saturday mornings. My sisters and I would migrate away from the TV and begin our other Saturday activities. My dad would take control of the TV and change the channels one clunk at a time. As I was making my escape, my dad would say something like, "Well I'll be dog gone. Would ya look at that. We're gettin' Peoria off the *side* of the antenna. Can you fathom that?"

The Christmas Junkie

At my present age, I enjoy Christmas a great deal, but as a child, I was a total Christmas junkie. As soon as Thanksgiving was over, I'd start walking around in a daze. I knew that Christmas was coming, and I loved everything about it.

In mid December, the whole family would pile into the Chevrolet Caprice Estate station wagon and take a trip to the Christmas tree farm. Upon arrival, my dad was usually in a good mood, but something always happened between arrival and departure. Everyone in the family had an opinion about which tree we should choose, and by the time we finally agreed on one, my dad would be totally disgusted.

I remember one year when it was very cold, and we were all tramping through knee-high snow at the Christmas tree farm. It was getting late in the evening, and Laura was becoming awfully heavy to carry. We all quickly agreed upon the first decent tree that we found. My dad cut it down and tied it to the top of the car. While setting it up at home, one of my sisters started complaining about a bare spot that she noticed on one side of the tree. My mom took a look at the bare spot, and she also expressed concern. My dad hated making mistakes.

He thought the family was blaming him for cutting down a defective tree. He got completely disgusted and went into his shut-down mode. He stopped talking, sat down in his chair, started reading a *Popular Science* magazine, and washed his hands of the whole thing.

My mom was even-tempered and great at smoothing over problems. She went outside and snipped a few branches out of the big pine tree in our backyard, then she used some wire and filled in the bare spot. After that, the whole family joined in to decorate the tree: all except for my dad. He stayed in his funk and refused to participate.

After decorating the tree, we always set up the nativity scene on top of our console television. My mom always called it "The Crèche," and she warned us to be careful with it. We had to unpack everything that had been carefully stored at the end of the previous Christmas season. Mary, Joseph, and baby Jesus were each individually wrapped in a sheet of year-old newspaper. It was the same for the wise men and the animals. I always enjoyed helping to set up the nativity scene. I had a definite opinion about how it should look. I thought the wise men should be standing in a line waiting their turn to bestow the gifts, and I thought all the animals should be looking toward baby Jesus. All except for one stubborn sheep who was grazing on some green grass in the middle of the desert and was too self-absorbed to look up from the ground. There was a shiny gold star included with the set. We always stuck the star at the peak of the roof on Jesus' barn, even though it didn't make much sense for a star to be on the roof. Where else are you going to put it?

Another one of my favorite holiday decorations was a Santa Claus doll about two feet high. We always unpacked Santa each year and posed him, in a sitting position, beneath the tree. I always thought Santa had a strange looking face. His eyes were a bit droopy, and he had an odd looking grin on his face. After several years of use, Santa developed a tear in his red suit. We could see a little bit of the stuffing, and it looked like newspaper. Jeny got curious and removed Santa's boot. She pulled the stuffing out of his left leg and unrolled the newspaper. We were all amazed to see the newspaper was covered with indecipherable Japanese characters. There was no doubt that our Santa Claus was *made in Japan.*

During December, after our house was decorated, I never wanted to leave the front room. I loved watching the lights twinkling on the Christmas tree. Sometimes I'd get up and move from one chair to another just to get a different perspective on the beautiful tree. Sometimes I'd crawl under the tree and look up at all the beautiful lights and decorations. My mom would say, "Why don't you check the water while you're down there?" I'd pull back the tree skirt and take a peek at the water level and report my findings. Sometimes we'd go and visit relatives at Christmastime. I was always appalled to see that my grandmother had no Christmas tree. After seventy or eighty Christmases, I guess the magic wears off, and it's not worth the effort anymore. I couldn't stand to ever see a dark Christmas tree. Every morning, when I came down stairs for breakfast, I'd go directly to the tree and turn on the lights. Several times I asked Mom to leave the tree lights on all night so that I could be greeted the next morning by a festive looking, fully illuminated tree; but she wouldn't go for it.

While waiting for the school bus, Jeny, Laura, and I would watch *The Garfield Goose Show* on WGN channel 9. Christmastime was wonderful on *The Garfield Goose Show.* Frazier Thomas would get out the little screen, hang it on the wall, and direct the audience to look closely as the camera zoomed in on it. Then my sisters and I would cheer when we heard Frazier Thomas say, "Have a look at *Hardrock, Coco, and Joe.*" It was a strange old cartoon about three of Santa's elves. They would sing a song about Christmas, and at the end of each stanza was the familiar part that we loved, "I'm Hardrock, I'm Coco," and then in a very deep voice, "I'm Joooooo."

At the start of the Christmas season, the merchants in Pontiac would sponsor *The Arrival of Santa Claus* event. It was the first day when Santa would setup shop in his little red house and start accepting requests from all the kids. All the families with small children would gather at the appointed place and time to see Santa arrive. One year, just to change it up a bit, Santa decided to forgo the sleigh and reindeer. Instead, Santa arrived in a real helicopter! I thought that was cool. I have subsequently heard a semi-famous song recorded by Gene Autry called, *Santa Claus is Coming in a Whirlybird.* I actually saw it happen in real life!

Each year Santa Claus occupied a little red house on the courthouse square in Pontiac. It was vitally important to make a visit in order to inform Santa about what I wanted. It was nice and warm inside his little house. I never wanted to seem greedy, so I only told him about one or two things that I wanted. For some reason, Santa always had bad breath, so I didn't waste any time chitchatting on his lap.

Some years, my dad would take Jeny, Laura, and I shopping in Pontiac without Mom, so that we could each get her something nice. Pontiac had ten or fifteen stores all around the courthouse square. At Christmastime, there were loud speakers at the corners of the square playing suitable holiday music. All of the stores would be decorated for Christmas. There was a clothing store that had some little mechanical reindeer turning their heads back and forth, and a mechanical Santa waving to all the passers by. I could never think of anything to buy Mom, so I usually resorted to perfume. She probably had a lifetime supply of Chanel No. 5 by the time I finally left the nest.

On Christmas morning, Jeny allowed Laura and I to look inside our Christmas stockings, but she wouldn't let us open any presents until Mom and Dad woke up. I was always bewildered to find an orange in my stocking. I couldn't imagine why Santa would give a kid an orange for Christmas. If I wanted an orange, all I had to do was open the refrigerator. And the walnuts were even more of a mystery. What kind of goofy kid wants walnuts in his Christmas stocking? I can just image some kid sitting on Santa's lap. The kid says, "I want Rock-em Sock-em Robots. I want a Johnny Lightning Race Car. But most of all, more than anything else, I really hope that you can bring me … some walnuts."

Testing, Testing, Is this Thing On?

Whenever my mom needed something of a hardware nature, she liked to go to Yordys' True Value Hardware Store in Pontiac. I also liked going to Yordys' because the floor squeaked in interesting ways, and they had a lot of manly stuff to look at. The fishing tackle was fun to peruse, and I also liked to look at the baseball gloves and the BB guns. It was such a relief to be in a store that actually had stuff that I liked, not like J.C. Penny: nothing but clothes, clothes, and more clothes.

While my mom was talking to the man about the high price of fluorescent lights, I happened upon an item that I just couldn't live without. It was a set of walkie-talkies. The package said that you could talk to someone a quarter mile away. The set was on sale for thirteen dollars. I had some lawn mowing money burning a hole in my pocket, which meant that I only needed to nag my mom for three bucks plus tax.

When I got the pair of walkie-talkies home, I opened the package and found the little instruction booklet. Before doing anything, I spent twenty minutes and thoroughly read every word. (My father raised me to be an avid instruction reader.) My next step was to install a battery in each of the hand held units. Luckily, when I opened the refrigerator, I found two of the square-shaped, nine-volt batteries that I needed. My mom had read somewhere that batteries lasted longer if you kept them in the refrigerator. We generally had a few of each size in the egg compartment. My friends were always amazed. "You keep *batteries* in your *refrigerator?*"

After installing the batteries, I turned one of the units on. I was happy to see a little red light begin to glow, and I was greeted by the sound of static. As I turned the little volume wheel, the static got louder and louder. I turned the other unit on, and it also sounded nice and static-y. Each walkie-talkie had two controls that were operated with your thumb. One was the on-off-volume wheel, and the other was the push-to-talk button. With both units turned on, I made my first attempt at sending a message over the airwaves. I pressed the push-to-talk button on one of the units and was treated to a loud and piercing squeal. The sound subsided when I let go of the button. My mom was alarmed. She hollered from the other room, "What was *that?*" I said, "Just feedback, Mom." I had thoroughly read the instructions, but I failed to follow them. When they said to keep the two units at least three feet apart, they meant it.

After I realized my mistake, I went looking for a sibling before making another test. The first one I found was Laura, and she agreed to help me. I told her to hold one of the units, and then I went to another room. I pushed the button and said, "Testing. Testing. Is this thing on?" Laura yelled through the wall, "It's working!" I hadn't taught her how to reply. After a short lesson, we were able to communicate with each other using the walkie-talkies. Laura stayed in her room, and

I began walking around the house. Our conversation was very limited.

"Can you hear me?"
"Yeah."
"Can you hear me now?"
"Yeah."
"OK, I'm going outside."
"Can you still hear me?"
"Yeah, where are you?"
"I'm clear out in the backyard."
"Wow!"
"Hold on, I'm going to keep walking."
"Where are you now?"
"I'm out by Debbie's apple tree."
"Wow!"
"Where are you now?"
"I'm walking down by the junkyard."
"Wow!"
"Can you still hear me?"
"Yeah."
"Can you hear me now?"
"Yeah."

When I got down near the Swygert Cemetery, the signal started getting weak. Each time Laura responded, I heard a lot of static mixed in with her voice. I decided that the cemetery must be a quarter of a mile away just like the instructions said. "The effective communication range of this True Value Tru-Tone walkie-talkie set is approximately one-quarter mile, depending upon the strength of the batteries and the atmospheric conditions." On my way back home, I could hear in Laura's voice that she was already losing interest. There was a little tone of exasperation in her answers every time I asked, "Can you still hear me?"

I decided that I was going to have to find a friend to play walkie-talkie, because Laura wasn't into it. I took both units over to Dale Cagley's house. I gave him a little lesson about how to use it, and then we separated from each other and began to talk. We tested the range by walking into different rooms of his house. Dale was completely captivated by my new toy. He kept pushing the button and saying things like:

"This is cool Utterback!"
"Yeah, I know."
"Where did you get these, man?"
"At Yordys' True Value."
"This is cool, man! I can't believe how great these things work!"
"Yeah, they go up to a quarter of a mile depending upon atmospheric conditions."
"Cool man, a quarter of a mile!"

I think it was Dale who finally broke the monotony. "Hey, Utterback, we ought to play spy with these things." Dale told me to stay at the base station, (his front porch) and he'd report his surveillance activities. With his back against the wall, Dale walked close to the side of his house and slowly slithered into the backyard.

"Cagley to base, I found something suspicious."
"What is it?"
"I discovered a black canine animal."
"10-4, it must be your dog, Cricket."

"Affirmative, man."

"10-4, keep me posted."

"Cagley to base, I see a very interesting subject."

"What is it?"

"I am setting up a stakeout on a female human being."

"10-4. Is it a suspicious character?"

"Yeah, man, very suspicious."

"Good work. What is the female doing?"

"Lying on a blanket in the backyard."

"Can she see you?"

"No man, she has her eyes shut."

"Can she hear you?"

"No man, I'm keeping my distance."

"Good work. Maintain surveillance on the suspect."

"Yeah man, I will post a stakeout at this vicinity."

"Base to Cagley. What is the suspect doing now?"

"Nothing man. Just lying in the sun."

"10-4. What is the suspect wearing?"

"A green bikini, man."

"10-4. What color is her hair?"

"Uh dark brown, I guess, man."

"10-4. How old is the suspect?"

"Approximately sixteen years of age."

"10-4. Which one of your foxy sisters is it?"

"HEY!"

"Oh, sorry."

"Base to Cagley. I have official instructions from the Commander?"

"10-4 man. Ready to receive instructions."

"Your mission, should you chose to accept it, is to sneak up behind the subject and pour cold water on her back."

"10-4. I will accept the mission."

"Proceed with care."

The next thing I hear is a high pitched girly scream lofted up and over the roof of the house. On the walkie-talkie I hear, "Abort the mission! My cover is blown, man! Evacuate the base-station!"

I jumped off the porch and left the vicinity and waited until the coast was clear.

Roasting Weenies and
Crashing Trains

~~~~~~

Our house in Swygert had a big yard and a lot of trees. Every windstorm created a nice crop of sticks and twigs to pickup. Anytime my mom saw me unoccupied, she'd say, "Would you like to go out and pick up some sticks for me?" (All of her commands were in the form of a question.) Aside from playing pick up sticks for my mom, I also helped my dad trim the trees whenever he noticed them getting shaggy. Every year I thought we were finally done, but we were never done. Those trees just kept on growing. Every time we trimmed another tree we'd throw the branches onto a big pile in the backyard. My dad said it was best to let the wood dry out, and it gave us an excuse to throw a weenie roast party in October.

The great thing about living out in the country is that there are no rules. If you want to have a bonfire in your backyard, then you just go ahead and do it. All summer long, our pile of sticks and branches would grow higher and higher. By the time October rolled around we always had a huge pile. It was usually taller than my dad, and he was a six-footer.

When the appointed day for the weenie roast arrived, I'd help my dad prepare for the guests. We'd set up folding chairs around the burn pile and also situate some big logs to sit on. I personally enjoyed sitting on the logs because it made the event feel more rustic. Another preparatory task was to create the weenie roasting sticks. We didn't use those store-bought metal skewers. We used the real thing. My dad taught me how to make them. First, we'd search around in the pile of branches to find a few suitable candidates. Next, we'd break off the superfluous twigs in an attempt to make some roasting sticks which weren't too long, too short, too thick, too thin, or too crooked. Then my dad would take out his Case pocket-knife, (he never went anywhere without it) and whittle the ends of the sticks down to a point. The whittling also served to debark the sticks and left a nice clean skewer for the hotdog.

As soon as the guests arrived, my dad would light the fire. He'd crinkle up some newspaper and stuff it into the pile. Then he'd take out his silver Zippo lighter (he never went anywhere without it) and light the newspaper. The newspaper would catch easily, and then the small twigs and branches would begin to burn. The pile was generally chocked full of dead leaves. The leaves always made a wonderful crackling sound. As more and more leaves caught fire, the flames expanded. There became a point of no return where the entire pile was flaming, and the sound of the crackling leaves became a tremendous roar. It only took a half-minute for all the leaves to be consumed, and I'd sometimes worry that the fire might go out, but if enough of the smaller sticks and branches were aflame, the fire could sustain itself. Then, during the next five or ten minutes, the amount of flames would once again expand until the entire pile was steadily burning with the red and yellow flames rising fifteen or twenty feet into the air. Everyone would take several steps back. The heat from a bonfire can be very impressive. Even from twenty feet away, you can feel it radiating on your face and hands. The adult chatter would decrease, and the kids would stop running all around. People would begin to stare into the flames. There's something special about a fire that make people quiet and thoughtful. The dancing flames act as a form of hypnosis.

Novice weenie roasters often have the misconception that the weenies should be roasted when the bonfire is at the height of its glory; but that's wrong. You must wait, sometimes an hour, for the flames to subside and the heat to reduce down to a tolerable level. When only a few substantial logs were left burning, my dad liked to use a garden fork to push what was left of the burning branches into a consolidated area for cooking purposes. There were always a lot of hot glowing embers that also worked well for cooking.

At this point, everyone would grab a roasting stick and get down to business. I enjoyed watching the different cooking methods that people used. The impatient kids generally stuck their hotdog into the hottest flame that they could find. After a few seconds, they declared it to be done and pulled it out of the fire to inspect the results: black and crusty on the outside and raw on the inside. Mothers would protest, "You can't eat that, it's burnt." Children would proclaim, "I like it that way."

The very young kids were allowed to hold their own roasting stick over the fire only after several choruses of, "Can I hold it? Can I hold it? Can I hold it?" No mater what precautions were taken, the hotdog would eventually make its way into the ashes. When that happened it was either blow it off, brush it off, or throw it in.

Some of the adults acted like gourmet hotdog roasters. They held their hotdog over the bright red embers in order to cook slowly. The adults would patiently hold and turn, hold and turn, hold and turn. The impatient kids wouldn't heed the parents' advice nor learn from their example. They insisted upon thrusting their hotdog into the biggest flame they could find. It all tasted the same to them.

After we had finished cooking, we'd all sit down to eat. There was always a wonderful selection of side dishes that the guests had brought to share. I enjoyed the side dishes as much, if not more, than the hotdogs. We always had potato salad, baked beans, cookies, cakes, and pies; and what would a weenie roast be without deviled eggs? It seems like there was always someone who brought a new dish that no one had ever heard of before. Items such as *Seven Layer Salad* and *Tollhouse Pan Cookies* were quite new and different when I was young. Often times, the name of a new dish took on the name of the person who first introduced it. *Jeny's Potatoes* are now famous in my family.

After filling up on all of the wonderful food, the adults would gather in a clump and do what else: talk. The kids never understood the big deal about sitting and talking, but it seemed to be the sole source of enjoyment for the adults. While the adults talked, we took the opportunity to go and mess around.

I remember one of our parties when my cousin from Graymont was in attendance. His name was David McDonald, and his family often came for visits to our house. David was three years older than I. This was just enough age difference so that he could teach me mischievous tricks that I hadn't thought of. The age difference also caused me to generally follow his lead. I naively associated age with wisdom.

On this particular day, David and I went walking around the yard after eating. We had a small ditch near our house that generally held a few inches of water. David got a bright idea that we should build a dam in the ditch. I'm not sure why he wanted to build a dam; maybe he had an interest in civil engineering. I gladly obliged him and got two shovels from the garage. When I returned, we both started shoveling dirt and gravel from the shoulder of the road into the ditch. We had just gotten started when my dad appeared on the scene. He was not happy. After a good bawling out, we were told to shovel the dirt and gravel back where we had found it. We quickly repaired the mess, and then we left the area in order to get as far away from my angry father as possible.

We next found ourselves walking around on the railroad tracks. I showed David a spot on the rail where I'd placed a penny several weeks before. I was expecting the train to flatten it out. When I went back to get my penny, I found that it was not only flat, but it had been squashed into the rail and had become permanently attached to it. It was so flat that it actually became part of the rail. There was no possible way to remove the penny.

After David heard this story and saw how the train had obliterated my penny, he began to wonder if the train could smash bigger things as well. He looked around and found a metal railroad spike lying nearby. He placed it on the rail. Then he began walking along the tracks picking up rocks and anything else he could find to place on the rail. After walking a few hundred feet, we came upon a big pile of discarded rusty railroad spikes. We both took a big handful of the spikes and began putting them on the tracks. He told me to come back tomorrow, after the train had passed, to see the results of our handiwork. I was excited to see what the train would do to all the stuff we put on the tracks. I was also worried that we may cause some harm to the train. Some of the stuff we put on the rails was pretty big. On the other hand, I never in my life heard of a train being derailed by debris on the tracks.

After we tired of our railroad activity, we went back to my house. We went down to the basement to play with my Aurora Model Motoring electric slot car racetrack. The slot car set was my most prized possession. It was more than a toy to me. It was more like a hobby. I spent a lot of time with my slot car track. It captured my imagination better than any other toy. I always showed it to my friends who came over to play. It was set up on an old table in the basement, and there was a pair of mismatched chairs to sit in while playing with the racetrack. There was something magical about sitting in front of the racetrack, down in the basement, watching the cars zoom around the circuit. The basement was always damp and cool, and I loved how the basement smelled. My mom said the smell was mildew, but I didn't care. It smelled great to me. Nobody went down to the basement except for my dad and me. I thought it was a manly place to hang out. My sisters never went down there. They thought it was creepy.

David and I sat quietly racing our cars around and around the track. Neither of us spoke much. I was still concerned about what we had done to the railroad tracks. The longer I sat there, the more concerned I got. I pictured in my mind a terrible train crash, and it would be our fault. I began to feel very scared and a little sick. I didn't want to voice my concern to David. I was afraid he'd call me a sissy or something. I noticed that David was very quiet too. Neither of us spoke. We just kept watching the cars go around and around. With each pass around the track, my fears grew stronger and stronger. I didn't want to be the cause of a train accident, but I also didn't want to be called a sissy. I kept checking his face for expression. I didn't know how he felt.

After a while, David broke the silence. He spoke quietly and seriously. He said, "I've been thinking about what we did. You don't suppose the train will crash, do you?" I was relieved that he was thinking along the same lines that I was thinking. It gave me permission to express my fear. I answered back quietly, "I don't know, but I'm really scared!" All the color had left both of our faces. David put down his slot car controller, pushed his chair back, and said, "Let's go."

His sentence was like a starter's pistol. We both jumped up and ran outside. The sun was very low in the sky, and it was nearly dark. We ran toward the railroad tracks and began clearing the debris. We couldn't see very well in the twilight, so we resorted to dragging our feet along the rails and kicking away all of the stuff that we could find. We worked very quickly because we were so scared. I felt better and better every time I kicked away another railroad spike. When we had cleared away everything we could find, we stopped to catch our breath. David asked, "Do you think we got 'em all?" I said I thought we had.

As we started walking back home, I felt very relieved. It was like a huge weight had been lifted from my shoulders. I felt so much better. When we got back to my house, David's family was about to leave. His Dad asked in a condescending tone, "What have you two been up to? ... Up to no good?" We didn't bother to answer. After averting a tremendous train crash, enduring a sarcastic remark is nothing. We just looked at each other with relieved faces. We never told anyone what we had done.

Over the River and
Through the Woods

~~~~~~

Grama Wilkins was my mom's mother. She lived in Paris, Illinois in a small house on Jefferson Street. By the time I came along, my mom's father had long since passed away, so I never got a chance to meet him. Grama Wilkins lived with her oldest son, George, my mom's big brother.

Every couple of months, we'd pack the whole family into our station wagon and go visit Grama and George in Paris. They lived two and a half hours away. It was a significant trip. When my sisters would tell their friends that we were going to Paris for the weekend, they were very impressed until they found out it was only Paris, Illinois.

Our car was a brown Chevrolet Caprice Estate station wagon with genuine, simulated, imitation, wood-grain trim. It was the kind of station wagon in which the third seat faced backwards. I loved riding in that rear-facing back seat. You couldn't see where you were going, but you certainly had an excellent view of where you'd been.

I remember riding in the rear-facing seat with my sister, Jeny. Jeny always had some sort of travel activity. She had a little gizmo that she made out of paper. It fit over the thumb and index finger of each hand. Jeny would say, "Pick a number." I'd say, "Three." She'd count "one, two, three." "Pick a color." "Green." "OK green. G-R-E-E-N." While she was counting and spelling, she'd be working her fingers back and forth with the little paper gizmo. Finally, after all the picking numbers and choosing colors and counting numbers and spelling colors, she'd stop and open the appropriate flap on the gizmo and read my fortune. It very accurately predicted vague and ambiguous facts about my future. I was very impressed.

Jeny also had a book of travel games for kids. One of the chapters instructed us to sing a song, and the lyrics were written in the book. It was a very long song, and I thought it would never end. Jeny and I would sit back there watching the world go by in reverse and sing this song. It goes to the tune of *Oh my Darling, Clementine*.

Found a peanut, found a peanut, found a peanut just now.
Just now, I found a peanut, found a peanut just now.
Cracked it open, cracked it open, cracked it open just now.
Just now, I cracked it open, cracked it open just now.
It was rotten, it was rotten, it was rotten just now.
Just now, it was rotten, it was rotten just now.
Ate it anyway, ate it anyway, ate it anyway just now.
Just now, I ate it anyway, ate it anyway just now.

The song goes on and on, mile after mile, and the peanut makes the kid sick, and the kid throws up, and I don't know what all.

Our station wagon had one radio speaker in the back Jeny was constantly pestering my dad to turn on WLS AM 89. They played all of the coolest rock and roll hits, and Jeny sang along with every song. She must have known the words to every hit song from 1965 to 1980. When a new song came out, it only took a few days until Jeny had every word memorized.

After making this trip to Paris every couple of months, year after year, I had the route memorized. First, we went through Fairbury and then Forrest (with two 'r's), and then Strawn, Sibley, and Gibson City. There was some kind of factory in Gibson City that smelled bad. The factory was extremely proud of its safety record. They had a big sign announcing that there hadn't been an accident at the factory in the last X number of days. I always looked forward to reading the sign as we passed through Gibson City: "Accident Free for 213 Days." Changing that sign everyday gave the safety manager something to do, I guess.

Gibson City also had a drive-in movie theater called, The Harvest Moon. We never actually stopped to see a movie, but if we passed by after dark, we could generally see about five seconds worth.

After Gibson City was a town called Mahomet, and then we left the two-lane road and got on the interstate highway. There were always several trucks on the highway. If a truck got behind us, Jeny and I would make that pull-the-rope arm motion out the back window. If the trucker tooted his air horn we'd cheer.

It was about this point in the trip when my mom would start asking if anyone wanted a drink of water. My mom had won a genuine blue and white Coleman thermos as a door prize at some sort of party. The thermos had a built-in plastic cup in the lid. Mom didn't want anyone to die of thirst on those long trips to Paris. She usually brought some cookies and crackers too.

After we finally made it to Paris, I'd start recognizing things as we came into town. There was a Burger Chef restaurant and also a Dog-n-Suds, but we never ate there. There was also a grocery store called Bridwell's. My mom always commented as we passed by Bridwell's, "That's the store where George walks to get groceries."

When we arrived at Grama's house, we'd park on the driveway in front of the one-car garage which never contained a car. George couldn't drive, and Grama gave up driving after she reached a certain age. We'd all pile out of the car and unfold our legs and bend and stretch a little. We never knocked on the door. We just walked right in.

After we got in the house, we'd each go and give Grama a peck on the cheek. It was an effort for her to stand up, so she didn't bother. She always sat in her special chair beside the telephone table. On the telephone table was a reading lamp, a great big magnifying glass, and a big clunky black telephone. Some good-samaritan thought he was doing Grama a big favor when he gave her an extra-long telephone cord. That long telephone cord was always terribly twisted into a horrendous jumble. On occasion, my dad would spend some time trying to untwist the telephone cord, but it was always a complete mess the next time we went to visit. My dad would say, "Well I swan. They couldn't twist it up any worse if they tried."

Grama Wilkins had diabetes and arthritis and probably a few other things. She used a walker on the rare occasions when she got up from her chair. Grama was a sweet lady with a warm and loving smile. Her most distinguishing feature was her feet. The big toe on her right foot emerged from the foot part in the normal manner, and then it took a sharp, ninety-degree turn to the east and crossed completely over the next toe. A few of the other toes were mangled and crossed in strange directions as well, and the left foot was just as bad. I was fascinated with Grama's feet. It was the same sort of fascination that makes people gawk at a wrecked car along the side of the road.

George was my mom's brother, and he lived with Grama Wilkins. George's hair was gray, and he always had a flat-top haircut. He was a bit overweight, and he wore his pants way up high over his belly. George had a strange speech pattern. I could never understand a single word he said. My mom always had to translate. I guess she had plenty of practice growing up with George. My mom said that George was the first born, and the doctor used forceps to get him out. It injured his brain. I don't think George ever made it past the fifth-grade. He never married, and he lived with Grama all his life.

George had a special rocking chair that he always sat in. It was next to the big picture window in the front room. He liked being by the window so he could see when the paperboy passed by. George loved to look at the newspaper, and he looked forward to receiving a new one each day. I was never quite sure if he really knew how to read, but that didn't stop him from enjoying his daily paper.

Another thing I remember about George is that he was constantly twisting his forearm back and forth. He'd sit and rock in his chair and twist that arm back and forth. Someone had bought George a self-winding watch. They thought they were doing him a big favor, so he wouldn't have to remember to wind it. The gift giver made the mistake of telling George that the watch winds itself using the natural everyday movement of your arm; so George would sit and twist his arm back and forth to make sure that he had plenty of natural everyday arm movements.

George had a collection of marbles. He kept them in the closet in a big metal cookie tin that had a lid on it. Right next to the marbles was a big old wooden Hop-Ching Chinese Checker board. Every time we went to visit Grama, I'd perform the obligatory greetings and sit down on the white couch just long enough to be polite, then, at the first opportunity, I'd go straight for the closet and bring out the marbles and the Chinese Checker board. I'd lay it down in the middle of the floor and then coax Laura to oppose me in a game.

The first step was for each player to find ten marbles of the same color. There were hundreds of marbles in the cookie tin, but after a little searching, it wasn't hard to find ten matching ones. After a few years of choosing the solid color green marbles every time, (my favorite color) I finally decided to mix it up a bit. I started using what my mom called the *cats-eye* marbles. Of course, I always used the green ones.

Laura was two years my junior, and she usually lost every game, but she didn't seem to mind. Sometimes Jeny would join us and we'd have a three-way match. If we were really lucky, we could sometimes coax a few other people to join in. It was possible to have a maximum of six people playing on that star-shaped board, and I think we actually did on a few occasions. With that many people playing, there was always a tremendous traffic jam in the middle of the board. In a case like that, I eventually learned the shortest route between two points is *not* a straight line. I marched my marbles in a big curved path in order to avoid the congestion.

Grama's favorite game to play was a card game called Flinch. The Flinch box was kept in the closet too. Sometimes on Saturday afternoons, Grama would play Flinch with us. She liked playing on a TV tray because she wasn't able to sit on the floor. Grama was a good Flinch player. She never missed a trick, and when it was her turn to play, she'd always say, "Now then … is it my time?" and George would say, "Yeow!"

In the kitchen, Grama always kept a bottle of clear liquid sitting on the table. The bottle had a white plastic top in the shape of a clarinet mouthpiece. It was some sort of special liquid sugar for diabetics. One time my mom let me put some on my breakfast cereal. It wasn't bad.

Grama had a garbage disposal in the kitchen sink. We didn't have one at home. My mom was a little afraid of it. Someone had told her that it was important to run water in the sink when using the garbage disposal. If anyone turned on the switch without running water in the sink my mom would have a conniption; and she was always petrified that a knife or spoon would fall in there.

Grama had a next-door neighbor named Mrs. Chively. There was some sort of arrangement whereby Mrs. Chively would do things for Grama and George, and I think she was paid for it. Each time we went to visit Grama, we always had to endure a half hour conversation about the things that Mrs. Chively was supposed to do but didn't, or the things that she wasn't supposed to do but did. My mom was very protective of Grama and George. She'd get upset hearing about this sort of thing, and then she'd make it a point to go and have a good talk with Mrs. Chively.

Grama Wilkins had cable TV. We were always amazed that she had thirteen channels; and every one was in perfect, crystal-clear, black and white! We only had four fuzzy channels at home: maybe five if the sky was clear. My dad liked to watch professional wrestling on Grama's TV. Those guys were brutal. They never followed the rules, and the referee was clueless.

Grama had a little shelf in the living room with various knickknacks and tchotchkes. There was a little bobble head Chinese boy and girl. The girl had a little magnet in her cheek, and the boy had a little magnet in his lips. If the boy was placed anywhere near the girl, he'd give her a kiss on the cheek. When you pulled them apart, they would resist until the magnets let go, and then both of their heads would wobble and bounce up and down. Laura and I were fascinated with this little Chinese couple. We couldn't resist playing with them even though we weren't allowed to. George appointed himself as the knickknack police. Whenever he saw our little hands reaching toward the Chinese couple he'd sound the alarm using his indecipherable George language, and my mom would come running.

Bedtime at Grama's was quite an ordeal. The process always started by retrieving the blow-up mattresses from Grama's closet. They were intended as swimming pool floats, but we used them for sleeping on the floor. There was a red one and a yellow one, and they both had a plastic-y smell. Along with the two blow-up mattresses, we also used the couch and the rollaway bed that Grama had for company. I was always eager to test my lung power on those blow-up mattresses. When my face got red, and I started to feel light headed, Mom would say, "Why don't you let me have a turn with that?"

My mom insisted that the couch and each blow up mattress should be made up with a proper bottom sheet and top sheet and plenty of blankets. It took an hour to get everything prepared, but it was nice to know that Mom cared so much about us. The next morning we had to reverse the process after breakfast. It took another hour to fold up the sheets, squeeze the air out of the mattresses, and roll away the rollaway.

Grama and George had a window air conditioner. The air conditioner was controlled with a set of push buttons: on, off, high, low, etc. One time the air conditioner broke down and a repairman came to fix it. The part that broke was a black thing that contained all of the silver push buttons. The repairman left the broken part, and George saved it for me. The next time we came to visit, George gave me the old part with all the buttons on it. He thought that I'd like to play with it. He was right. I really liked that thing. If you pushed down one button, the one next to it would pop up. If you pushed down another button, the previous one would pop up. With all those buttons, it reminded me of a trumpet. I'd hold it near my face and make a trumpet sound with my mouth and push the various buttons.

When we got home, I showed my friend Dale Cagley. I told him my uncle gave me a new kind of trumpet. I must have made a pretty convincing trumpet sound because he was very impressed. His eyes got wide, and his mouth dropped open. He actually thought I was playing that thing. He couldn't believe it. He asked me if I ever had any trumpet lessons, and I said no. I couldn't believe he fell for it. It was hard for me to keep a straight face. I never knew that I had the ability to actually pull off a trick like that. I played another little tune for him. I thought he'd catch on, but he was thoroughly convinced. When he started acting jealous about my new found ability, I couldn't hold out any longer. I finally broke down and told him the truth.

Little Yellow Motorcycle

One of our frequent trips to visit Grama Wilkins stands out in my memory. It was a sunny Saturday morning. My dad was sitting next to my mom on Grama's white couch reading the want-ads in the *Paris Beacon News*. The rest of us were sitting on the floor watching *Underdog* cartoons on Grama's TV. She had cable, and we really enjoyed that clear black and white image. We even enjoyed watching the commercials. When the Culligan Water commercial came on, with that annoying lady who always yelled, "Hey Culligan Man," I noticed my dad speaking in low tones to my mom, and then he got up from the couch. As he opened the front door to go out, Grama asked, "Where are you going, Dean?" My dad, who never gave a straight answer to anyone, not even to little old ladies, said, "I'm going to see a man about a dog." Grama took him serious. She was convinced that he went to buy a dog. My mom told her that he was just pulling her leg.

My dad disappeared for an hour or so. When he came back, he was in a good mood. He told me he needed help with something, and I followed him out to our station wagon. We drove a few blocks and stopped in front of a house that I was unfamiliar with. There was a friendly looking guy standing in the side yard polishing a little motorcycle. My dad seemed to know the man, and they started talking to each other. The man was pointing to various levers and buttons on the motorcycle and telling my dad about one thing and another. I got the feeling that my dad had met the man during his earlier disappearance. I still had no idea why we were there. That was not unusual. My dad never wanted to waste any words unnecessarily. I knew I'd find out eventually. I certainly didn't dare to ask.

The motorcycle was cute and yellow and less bulky than those Harleys that I had seen. The engine looked small, but it was still a substantial motorcycle: big enough for adults to ride. I noticed the nameplate said "Honda Trail 90." I had heard of Honda motorcycles from friends at school and from seeing commercials on TV. I noticed that the tires were knobby. It looked like it could be ridden on trails as the name implied.

The man was telling my dad that he used to take the motorcycle with him on camping trips. He said that he made a little box for the back of the motorcycle and his dog liked riding back there. My dad thought that was funny. He smiled and said, "Is *that* right?" I was glad to see my dad in a good mood for a change.

The man unscrewed a knob on the side of the motorcycle and opened a little door. He showed us a little tool kit that was in there. The man explained that they were all metric tools, and that a person could supposedly take apart the entire motorcycle with that little tool kit. They both chuckled at the absurdity, because it was such a small tool kit. My dad once again smiled and said, "Is *that* right?"

The man showed my dad a little white lever down near the rear wheel. He said the lever was used to put the transmission into super-low gear for real rough terrain. My dad said, "Super-low huh? Just about have to drive a stake in the ground to see if it's moving." The man laughed, but I'm not sure if he understood my dad's comment. I didn't understand half of the things he said, and I didn't really expect anyone could.

The man pointed out a little black knob near the engine that had some tiny writing on it. He said you're supposed to pull that knob out if you're using the motorcycle at 5000 feet above sea level. My dad smiled and said, "I'll keep that in mind the next time I go to Mount Everest," and they both laughed again.

The man showed us that the motorcycle had two different kickstands. One was similar to a bicycle kickstand. The other was more substantial and took a bit of effort to use it. You had to hold it down with one foot and pull the whole motorcycle backwards about six inches. The kickstand supported the motorcycle vertically, and the rear wheel actually left the ground an inch or two.

During all of this explaining and pointing out one thing and another, I started to get a funny tingling feeling in my stomach. My tummy suspected something that hadn't yet made its way to my brain. My brain knew how frugal and practical my dad was. My brain knew that he'd never, in a million years, buy a motorcycle. Nevertheless, my brain had no control over my stomach, and my stomach continued to tingle. It was the true definition of a gut feeling.

Then, the man started to explain the necessary steps to start the engine. He showed us how to turn the gas lever on. He explained that the gas lever had three positions: on, off, and reserve. He said the reserve position would give you another ten miles or so, if you run the main tank dry. My dad laughed and said, "In case you run out of gas in the middle of the Mojave Dessert." The man laughed. Then the man explained other preparatory steps such as setting the choke, turning on the key, and squeezing the hand brake. Then he told my dad to go ahead and start it up. I was amazed to see my dad climb aboard and straddle the motorcycle. He unfolded the kick-start lever, just as if he had done it a thousand times before. My stomach began to tingle like crazy.

My dad stood upon the foot peg and then jammed down with all his weight on the kick-start. The engine began to run on the first try. I was very impressed. My dad was cooler than I ever thought he was. (I subsequently learned that my dad had some sort of motorbike when he was a teenager, so that accounts for his abilities.)

While the engine was running, the man put his face up close to my dad's ear and shouted some final instructions. My dad put the motorcycle in gear and began to drive around the man's backyard. The man nodded his approval, and my dad made several circles around the yard. I didn't know my dad could ride a motorcycle. My opinion of him ratcheted up a couple of notches.

My brain began to let some hope creep in, but I was still very skeptical. The whole thing was crazy. This was not my dad. He'd never spend money on something so frivolous. My dad only bought useful things. I never knew him to ever spend money on something like this. But my stomach wouldn't be denied. It continued to tingle away. The tingle had now increased into a rolling boil.

My dad drove the motorcycle back to the original spot and turned off the key. He looked in my direction with a grin on his face and said, "Well what do you think, son?" I didn't know what to say. I wondered if it was some sort of trick question. My brain raced through about ten or twenty possible responses. I wanted to say, "*Think about what? What the heck is going on here?*" but I didn't dare. I finally just smiled back and said, "Real nice!"

Apparently, that was an acceptable answer. I heard not a hint of sarcasm in my dad's next question. "You think we ought to take it home?" My dad could see that I was amazed and bewildered and a thousand other things. It was a given fact that any preteen boy would, of course, absolutely love to have a motorcycle in the family, and I was no exception. It was all happening so fast. I was surprised and confused by the whole thing. I had never heard my dad express any interest in buying a motorcycle before. I'm sure that my eyes got wide, and my face lit up, as I gave my one word response: "Sure!"

After that, it was all a blur. My dad and the man took care of some paperwork, and then they both figured a way to drain all of the gas out of the motorcycle. My dad was planning to load it into the station wagon, and he didn't want any gas leaking out. It wasn't the kind of motorcycle that you could ride on a two and a half hour trip all the way home to Swygert. We managed to get it into the station wagon, but it was a very tight squeeze. We had to lay down the second and third row of seats. We had to loosen the motorcycle handlebars and twist them at an odd angle. It took all three of us, but we somehow managed to get it in.

On the short ride back to Grama's house, Dad warned me not to tell her and George about our special cargo. He was afraid she wouldn't approve. I kept my mouth shut, but I went through the rest of the day in a daze with the knowledge that our car held a wonderful treasure. We discretely clued-in my mom and sisters. We didn't want them to be totally shocked when we saddled up to go home.

The ride home was quite a challenge. Luckily, Debbie and Joyce were out of the nest by this time, so we only had to squeeze in two adults and three kids rather than five. Jeny, Laura, and I, were on our best behavior. There wasn't a single complaint all the way home. What's two and a half hours of discomfort when you have a new motorcycle in the family?

On the way home, sitting in a strange position beside the motorcycle, I had wonderful visions of flying down the country roads around Swygert on the little yellow motorcycle. It was typical for farm kids to learn how to drive motorized vehicles at a young age. I started mowing the lawn using our Yardman riding lawnmower when I was in second-grade. It wasn't uncommon to see twelve year old farm boys driving tractors and pulling wagonloads of grain to the elevator. I knew several country friends who had go-karts and mini-bikes. With all of this in mind, it was certainly within the realm of possibility that my dad would teach me how to drive the motorcycle. I was only in fifth-grade, but it was a small, 90 cc trail bike, and I thought that I could handle it. I didn't have the impression that the motorcycle would exclusively belong to my dad. It seemed as if he intended it to be a family motorcycle.

When we got home, we all helped my dad take the motorcycle out of the car. We stored it in the breezeway: a sort of porch that was connected to the garage. Dad gave us firm instructions to leave the motorcycle alone, but there were also some encouraging hints. I got the impression that he was planning to give us rides on the weekend, and maybe even teach Jeny and me how to drive it. I told all my friends at school that we had a motorcycle, and my dad was going to teach me how to drive it. I don't think they believed me.

When my dad was at work, I'd go and sit on the little yellow trail bike and imagine what it would be like cruising down the road with the wind in my hair. I studied all of the gauges and indicators. I squeezed the hand brake. I examined all of the levers and switches that the man in Paris had talked about. I tried to remember everything he had said. The black knob with the tiny writing was for riding in mountains. The gas shut-off had a special position for the reserve tank. The little white lever in the rear was for super-low gear.

I remembered the little tool kit that the man in Paris had showed us. I got brave and decided to open the utility compartment. I didn't know if my dad would approve, but I couldn't help myself. I pulled out the little tool kit. All the tools were wrapped in a little plastic pouch. I unrolled the pouch and laid out all the tools on the floor. I sat looking at the little wrenches and screwdrivers. I laid out each wrench in order from biggest to smallest. I noticed the size of each wrench was written in whole numbers like 12, 10, 8, and 7. It was completely different from the normal 7/8ths, and 9/16ths that I was used to. I remembered the man had said they were metric tools, and I considered them to be cool and exotic. I imagined that if the motorcycle ever broke down far from home, I could get out the little tool kit and fix it. I made a mental note to tell all my friends about the metric tools, and then I carefully packed the tools back into the pouch. I placed the pouch back in its place, and then I closed up the utility compartment. I sincerely hoped that my dad would be none-the-wiser.

As it turned out, Swygert was an excellent place to live for trail bike riding. At first, my dad was the sole driver, and he gave rides to each family member. Even my mom took a ride, and she came home with a muffler burn on her thigh. She must have been hanging on tight with her arms and legs and everything. After a few weeks, Dad taught Jeny and me how to drive it. We certainly weren't driving age, but Dad didn't think we could get into trouble if we stayed on the gravel cemetery road.

Jeny and I took turns. When she was driving, I rode on the back. When I was driving, she rode on the back. We made countless trips from our house to the cemetery and then back home again. It was about a quarter mile each way. The motorcycle had four gears. Dad taught us how to listen to the engine and watch the speedometer and shift at the appropriate times. When Jeny was riding behind me, she liked to say, "mmmmm and shift … mmmmm and shift." When I was riding behind Jeny, I'd give her my imaginary race commentary: "and Richard Petty enters the short shoot in second gear then shifts into third on his way into turn-two here at the Daytona International Speedway."

After we got tired of just riding back and forth to the cemetery, we got brave and decided it would be OK to actually enter the cemetery. The cemetery had a 'U' shaped road that ran through it. We could enter the cemetery and follow the road, and it would take us right back out again. We liked that because we never had to actually stop the motorcycle to turn around. Jeny sternly warned me to go slow in the cemetery to show our respect for the dead. We never went in during the rare occasions when a parked car indicated that someone was visiting a grave.

One day we saw Myron and Diane Burton riding a strange white motorcycle up and down the gravel cemetery road. Jeny and I were a little miffed. We thought they had stolen our idea. Myron and Diane were similar in ages to Jeny and me. Their father, Joe Burton, was a collector of antiques. He had a shiny old Ford automobile with a rumble seat that he drove in parades. I guess Joe happened to buy an old Cushman motorcycle somewhere. It was a little strange looking. Rather than having foot pegs, it actually had little running boards for your feet. It also had a loud engine, and it only had two gears. The gearshift was operated by hand using a big silver knob up near the gas tank.

Myron and Diane invited Jeny and me to ride with them. The four of us spent endless hours riding up and down the cemetery road: Jeny and I on our Honda, Myron and Diane on their Cushman. Sometimes the Cushman took the lead and sometimes the Honda took the lead. Even though we were kids, we all realized the danger and there was no horsing around. We just cruised back and forth at a sensible speed and had a lot of fun. The Cushman had a bigger engine, but the Honda was much quicker off the line. When Jeny and I took the lead, we could easily pull away from the Cushman in a short distance, but the Cushman could catch up if it had enough road.

Jeny and I treasured the little Honda Trail 90, and we continued to use it and enjoy it all during our teen years. My dad also enjoyed riding the little trail bike on the country roads, and I think Laura even drove it when she got older. We were so fortunate to have permissive parents. They didn't mind us riding the motorcycle as long as we stayed close to home. I'm so thankful for my parents' attitude. It allowed me to have a childhood that was rich with experiences and gave me thousands of pleasant memories of my youth.

Red Neck Kids Club: 4-H

When I was young, the 4-H Club was a big deal for a lot of the families who lived in the rural areas. It was sort of like Scouts for the farm kids. There were several local 4-H Clubs scattered around Livingston County, and every summer a three-day 4-H Fair was held at the 4-H Fair Grounds near Pontiac. Everyone in my family was involved in 4-H in one way or another. My mom was a 4-H leader for a while, my dad volunteered to work at the fair, and my sisters and I were all 4-H members.

There was a local 4-H Club that met once a month in the Owego School gym, only a mile and a half down the road from our house. Each local 4-H Club was required to have an official club name. The name of this one was *Owego Get 'em*. (Isn't that clever: oh we go get 'em.) Officially, the Owego Get 'em Club was chartered as a Boys 4-H Club, but there were a lot of girls in it. Apparently, the Boys 4-H Club had no rules against girls joining, and in the 1970's everything was switching to co-ed.

My sister, Jeny, was a member of the Owego Get 'em Boys 4-H Club. She was four years older than I was, and I generally wanted to do whatever she was doing. I was too young to join 4-H, and I was always disappointed each month when Jeny went to the 4-H meeting without me. My mom felt sorry for me and sent me to a few of the meetings as a visitor. Jeny was left with the embarrassing duty of explaining to the 4-H leader when he asked, "What is your little brother doing here?"

I remember that each 4-H meeting began with a lot of kids standing around and shooting baskets. I liked that part. There always seemed to be a good fifteen or twenty minutes worth of basketball shooting time while waiting for the late comers to arrive, and waiting for the 4-H leader to stop jawing with whichever parent was elected to bring the refreshments that month.

After a while, the 4-H leader would tell everyone to put the basketballs away and get down to business. Then the 4-H officers would set up a table in the middle of the gym floor with the American Flag on the right and the 4-H Flag on the left. All of the 4-H members would grab a chair and face the officers' table. The 4-H officers were responsible for running the meeting, but the 4-H leader never hesitated to jump in if there was any snag in the proceedings. The 4-H officers consisted of a president, vice president, secretary, treasurer and maybe a few others. During the first 4-H meeting of each year, the 4-H members would elect a new set of officers.

The 4-H meetings were conducted using a lot of formality. I was fascinated with the strict procedures that were followed. The president always had an official looking gavel lying on the table in front of him just like a judge in court. The president would bring the meeting to order and tap his gavel on the table a few times. I always hoped he'd pound hard on the table in a strong, authoritative manor, but he just wasn't a strong, authoritative type of guy. We had to settle for a few timid taps.

After the gavelling, the president would ask the secretary to read the minutes from the previous meeting. After the secretary had read all of the fascinating goings-on from last month, the president would ask if any member would like to make a motion to accept the minutes. One of the 4-H members would say, "I move to accept the minutes." Then someone else would say, "I second the motion." Then the president would ask all those in agreement to signify by saying "aye" and then all those opposed to signify by saying "no." (Nobody ever said no.) After that, the whole process repeated over again for the treasurer's report, the old business, and the new business. No one ever brought up any new business except for the 4-H leader, who generally had some new memo from the extension office that he wanted to discuss. When the 4-H leader started talking about the new business, a lot of squeaking of chairs and shuffling of feet would begin as all of the 4-H members started wondering when this thing would be over so they could all get back to shooting baskets.

After the formal meeting was over, we generally had refreshments. One of the mothers would bring Kool-Aid and cupcakes, or perhaps, if we were lucky, snicker-doodles. The boys would all wolf down their snack and head straight for the basketball hoops. The girls would gather in a little girly clump and talk about their girly stuff. At nine o'clock, the meeting would be over, and the parents would all come and pick up the kids.

As soon as I was old enough to officially join the 4-H Club, I signed up without hesitation. I didn't want to pass up a chance to shoot baskets on the second Tuesday of each month. I also thought that it would be pretty cool to become one of those officers. I thought it might be presumptuous to try for president on my first year in the club, but I had my eye on that treasurers position. I thought it would make a good steppingstone to start small and work my way up. Besides that, when I was attending meetings with Jeny as a visitor, I noticed that the treasurer didn't have to say much. The treasurer's report was generally only one sentence long. "We have one-hundred and sixteen dollars and forty-two cents."

On the second Tuesday of September, the first meeting of the 4-H fiscal year, the 4-H leader asked if anyone was interested in running for office. There was dead silence. Everyone looked at each other and shuffled their feet. After waiting for what I thought was an appropriate amount of time, I shyly raised my hand and said that I was thinking about becoming the treasurer. After I broke the ice, a few of the other kids started nominating each other. I was a little embarrassed that I had nominated myself, but it all worked out. We ended up with a full slate of candidates, and the voting part was easy, because each officer ran unopposed.

After being elected as the treasurer, the previous treasurer handed me a little box containing the checking account statements, the check register, and a partially used book of blank checks. I was proud to be entrusted with all this important stuff. I noticed that each blank check had the official account information in the upper left corner. It said in big bold letters: Owego Get 'em 4-H Club. Apparently, the stuffy people at the Pontiac National Bank had no rules against printing slang terms such as "'em" on the checks.

The 4-H organization had a goal of producing well-rounded kids with good self-esteem who could feel comfortable speaking in front of an audience. Each 4-H meeting was supposed to contain a talk, a demonstration, or an entertainment. These items were to be presented by one or more of the 4-H members, and generally took place directly after the formal meeting and before the refreshments. When I had been a visitor with Jeny, I remember seeing Bryant Fraher perform an out of tune trumpet solo, and I also remember sitting through a talk in which one of the farm girls stood up and fumbled through her three-by-five index cards, as she discussed the importance of hog vaccination.

During this first meeting of the year, the 4-H leader brought up the issue of the talks, demonstrations, and entertainments. He said that in previous years we had become lax, but this year he was going to crack down. Most kids would rather break an arm than to stand in front of an audience. When I was visiting with Jeny, we often had several meetings in which no talk, demonstration, or entertainment took place, but this year the leader indicated that things would be different. He said every 4-H member was required to sign up on the sign-up sheet. He said he wasn't going to stand for any last minute excuses or sudden illnesses, and he instructed the elected secretary to call and remind each poor soul a week or so in advance. (In any organization the secretary ends up doing all the work.)

When the sign-up sheet came to me, I wrote my name in a blank space as far in the future as I could find. After that, the meeting proceeded as usual. We ate our cupcakes and snicker-doodles and shot baskets until it was time to go home. I started to develop a dislike for a kid named Roger Lutz. He was a couple of years older than I was. Every time I managed to rebound a ball, Roger would sneak up behind me and steal it away, just when I started to dribble.

After the meeting, when I got home, I told my mom that I was elected as the treasurer. I showed her the contents of the little box. She noticed that there were only about three or four blank checks left in the checkbook, and she told me that I should ask them about it at the next meeting.

On the second Tuesday of October, I waited excitedly during the reading of the minutes and the motioning to accept the minutes and the seconding of the motion and the signifying by saying "aye" and the other preliminary stuff, and then, finally, the president asked for the treasurer's report. I stood up and said, in my strong authoritative treasurer's voice, "We have one-hundred and sixteen dollars and forty-two cents." Then I sat back down. I heard the 4-H leader snickering when the president called for a motion to accept my once sentence treasurer's report. I thought about mentioning the thing that my mom wanted me to mention, but I decided it was more proper to wait until it was time for the new business.

After the old business was dealt with, the president asked for the new business. I stood up and explained that we only had three or four blank checks left in the checkbook. I saw some concerned faces. The previous treasurer stood up and said that he also noticed that problem, but he decided not to worry about it because the club rarely ever had the occasion to actually write a check. After more discussion and concerned faces, the 4-H leader finally suggested that it would be a good idea to get some more checks. Some farm kid stood up and made a motion that we should ask the bank for green safety checks. He said his dad had green safety checks, and they were really cool. Someone seconded the motion for green safety checks, and then all those in agreement signified by saying "aye," and nobody was opposed, so the president declared that the motion was carried. He gave me the green light to get some green checks.

The next time we went into town, my mom took me to the bank, and we ordered some green safety checks. I couldn't believe that the bank actually charged money for blank checks. My mom indicated that it was standard operating procedure to charge for checks, but she was appalled that green safety checks cost two dollars more than the normal yellow ones. I told her, "We must get the green ones because *the motion carried*." After the bank deducted the price of the green checks from our account, I started practicing the new treasurers report for next month. "We have one-hundred and eight dollars and forty-two cents."

On the second Tuesday of November, we shot baskets like usual, and I once again delivered my one-sentence treasurers report. When the time came for the old business, I proudly stood up and showed all the members our new box of green safety checks. During the new business, the 4-H leader suggested that maybe we deserved to spend a little money and make use of one of those new green safety checks. He suggested some sort of Christmas outing for the December meeting. After some discussion, someone made a motion to go bowling, and the motion was seconded, and all those in agreement said "aye," and nobody was opposed, so the motion carried.

On the second Tuesday of December, we skipped the normal meeting, and all of the 4-H kids showed up at the bowling alley in Pontiac. It was the first time that I ever bowled in my life. I only had two or three gutter balls, and my final score was 106. When the festivities were over, it was my job, as treasurer, to write out a check and pay for our evening of fun. It was the first time in my life that I had ever written a check. The 4-H leader coached me along, and I could hear Roger Lutz laughing when I asked, "How do you spell forty?" (To this day, I don't understand why there is no 'u' in the word forty.)

On the second Tuesday of January, it was my turn to present a demonstration. When I had signed up for January on the sign-up sheet, I thought it was far enough away that it would never actually occur; but it did. The secretary called to remind me a week ahead of the meeting, and I reluctantly began to prepare. There were no rules about the subject matter for a demonstration. You were free to demonstrate anything that you wanted to demonstrate. I had been playing the snare drum for a couple of years, and I decided that it would be a good idea to give a demonstration entitled, *How to Play a Snare Drum*. After the reading of the minutes and the treasurer's report and the old business and the new business, I set up my snare drum in front of the officer's table and began my demonstration. I showed them the various parts of the drum. I showed them the top and bottom drum heads. I showed them the drum key used to tighten the heads. I showed them the snares on the bottom side. I explained how to tighten and loosen the snares. I demonstrated how to hold the sticks. I demonstrated how to strike the drum. I tried to impress them with technical snare drum jargon when I demonstrated how to play a flam, a ruff, a paradiddle, and a ratamacue. I demonstrated how to bounce the sticks. I demonstrated how to play a double stroke drum roll, and then my demonstration was over. I made it through the demonstration fairly well, except for the fact that my left kneecap was uncontrollably twitching up and down throughout the whole thing. I hoped that nobody could notice it nervously twitching away beneath my blue jeans.

On the second Tuesday of February, it was my turn to present the entertainment. The secretary called to remind me a week ahead, and this time, I already knew what kind of entertainment that I would present. I decided to entertain the 4-H members with a *Snare Drum Solo,* of course. After the reading of the minutes and the treasurer's report and the old business and the new business, the kids saw me bringing my snare drum to the front. I heard Roger Lutz grumbling, "Didn't he just do that last month?" Then, I had the embarrassing duty to explain that last month was a *demonstration* and this month is an *entertainment.* It was entirely two different things. After saying that, I still saw a lot of puzzled looks. Even the 4-H leader looked confused, but I went ahead and set up my snare drum and music stand, and I opened my *Rubank Intermediate Method for Snare Drum* book to the page containing the piece that I had chosen to perform. It was a substantial piece of snare drum music in 6/8 time that sounded like a military marching band cadence. I played it well with no mistakes. I played all the accents and performed all of the crescendos and diminuendos just as they were written in the music. As I approached the big finish at the end of the song, I was feeling very good about myself. It felt great to know that I had done a good job. After I finished playing, I sensed that everyone was rather impressed. There was a sincere smattering of applause, and I saw a smile on the 4-H leader's face.

As I was putting my music away, the 4-H leader stood and thanked me for the wonderful entertainment and coaxed the audience to applaud once again. He said, "It was *much* better than last month!" I forced out a smile and angrily thought to myself, "Last month was a *demonstration*. This month was an *entertainment*. Why can't anybody get that through their thick skull!"

The 4-H leader asked me the name of the snare drum solo that I had just performed. I was hoping nobody would ask me that. I had purposely omitted telling them the title of the piece. My face turned red, and my left kneecap began to twitch. I was forced to confess that it was not technically a *solo*. I confessed that I had chosen to play one-half of a *duet*, and the actual title of the song was, *The Two of Us*. That brought forth a lot of laughs, and I could hear Roger Lutz scoffing, "*The Two of Us*. … Ha. … He played a duet all by himself. … What a doofus." As I was putting my drum away, I felt all of that good 4-H self-esteem draining out onto the floor.

On the second Tuesday of March, the 4-H members entered the Owego School gym and noticed something new. There was a volleyball net stretched across the basketball court from one wall to the other. Since I was a student at Owego School, I knew the reason for the net. We had a new teacher who was a real go-getter. She thought that instead of playing basketball everyday, the students needed to broaden their horizons and try a new sport. She persuaded the PTA to buy a volleyball net, and she imposed upon the custodian to drill holes into the concrete block wall in order to screw in some eye-bolts to anchor the net. After that, she taught the students all of the rules of the game, and we began playing volleyball during recess instead of basketball.

The 4-H members apparently liked the new net. Some of them began playing volleyball instead of shooting baskets. They seemed to know the rules, but they didn't play exactly the same way that my teacher had taught us. For example, I was appalled when the 4-H kids served the ball without first announcing the score.

After ten or fifteen minutes of volleyball, the formal meeting began. Then we sat through a fascinating talk about root worm, and we were also treated to an entertainment in which one of the talented farm boys performed all three of the card tricks that he knew. After the refreshments, the 4-H leader suggested that we divide up into teams and play volleyball. The 4-H leader joined us and played on one of the teams.

After the first game began, I was impressed that the 4-H kids actually knew how to play something other than basketball. When it was my turn to serve, I did it exactly the way that my teacher had taught us in school. In a loud voice, I announced the score making sure to first say the score of the serving team and then the score of the opposing team. I said, *"Eleven … Fourteen … Service!"* As I served the ball over the net, I heard some snickering. Roger Lutz scoffed, *"Service!?!?"*

My serve was successful, and so I got to serve again. I knew the other kids were making fun of me, but I insisted upon serving the ball the way that my teacher had taught us. I said once again, *"Twelve ... Fourteen ... Service!"* This time, as I served the ball over the net, the other kids were anticipating my announcement. I heard loud roars of laughter. A few of the kids on the other team actually laid down on the floor and rolled with laughter. The 4-H leader was on my team, and he was embarrassed for me. As he handed me the ball for my third serve, he said, "OK Jeff. Just hit the ball over." I suppose he was trying to tell me to leave out the announcement, but I was adamant. I insisted on serving the correct way. I said, *"Thirteen ... Fourteen ... Service!"* Thankfully, this time, someone on the other team hit the ball back, and it dropped on our side of the net, so my turn to serve had ended, and the 4-H leader could stop acting so embarrassed.

Every year in June, with 4-H Fair time drawing near, we always had a special meeting that was held outdoors on a Saturday. This was the last 4-H meeting of the 4-H fiscal year. There wouldn't be any more meetings until September. The purpose of the special meeting was to take the official annual 4-H Club picture that would be used for the official annual 4-H Club wall calendar. The parents were also invited to this special meeting, and we always had the official annual 4-H Club picnic after the picture taking.

As my family was preparing to go to the special meeting, I came down stairs wearing my usual blue jeans and sneakers. My mom said, "It's really hot out there, why don't you wear your new shorts and sandals." She never wanted anyone to be hot, and she wanted me to look nice for the group picture. I protested, but she insisted, and so I went back up stairs to change.

When we arrived at the special meeting, I was horrified to see that I was the only geeky kid in the entire 4-H Club with shorts on. Everyone else was wearing blue jeans: even the girls. The 4-H Club was full of farm kids, and farm kids do not wear shorts. Every year my mom always hung the annual 4-H Club calendar in a prominent place on the wall in the kitchen. I had to look at myself for an entire year wearing those goofy plaid shorts.

When the 4-H Club recommenced again in the fall, I was a seventh-grader, and I no longer attended Owego Elementary School. I went to the Junior High in Pontiac. I tried out for the seventh-grade basketball team and just barely made it by the skin of my teeth. I was rather tall for my age, and the coach thought there might be some hope to turn me into a basketball player. I was designated as the third string center. During every game, I sat on the bench next to the other bench warmers. The only time I got to play was if we were winning by a large margin and I could do no harm, or if we were losing by a large margin and there was no hope.

We had basketball practice everyday after school for two hours. We ran wind sprints and practiced layups and free throws. We learned how to use back-spin on the ball and how to use the bank board. We learned how to box-out the opponent and how to make maximum use of your pivot foot. We learned how to implement a two-one-two zone defense and how to use a pick-and-roll maneuver when faced against a man-to-man defense. I absorbed everything I could learn from the coach, but I was never able to rise above my original position as the third string center.

At one of the winter 4-H meetings, the weather was bad, and only a few kids showed up. The only people shooting baskets were Roger Lutz and me. After a few minutes, he asked me if I wanted to play one-on-one. I accepted. Roger assumed he would kick my butt, and judging from my lack of success on the seventh-grade basketball team, I didn't really have any great expectations. After all, I was just a geeky kid that wore plaid shorts and played snare drum duets all by himself.

All those hours of seventh-grade basketball training made no improvement in my prospects on the seventh-grade team, but I was amazed to see that it really paid off against Roger Lutz. When he had the ball, I put up a tough defense that he was unable to penetrate. When I had the ball, I dribbled around him like he was standing still. I made bank shots and layups. Every shot I took went right in the basket. I amazed myself. I didn't know if it was just luck, or if I had actually learned something from the coach.

Every time I scored, I could see a little change on Roger's face. His condescending grin faded little by little. Every time I blocked his shot or stole the ball, I sensed a little more respect from him. It felt so good to pay him back for all those sneers and scoffs that he had hurled at me over the years. I felt some of that good 4-H self-esteem coursing through my veins.

Roger and I had agreed to play using the standard farm kid rules: first one to twenty wins. Toward the end of the game, I was leading by eight points. There was no doubt that I would win. Just before taking my final shot, I yelled, "*Eighteen ... Ten ... Service!*" and then I admired my shot as the ball arched toward the basket and made a perfect swish.

Oh Cripes, You got a Tape Recorder

〰〰〰〰〰〰〰〰〰〰〰〰〰〰〰〰〰〰〰〰〰〰〰〰〰〰〰〰

One year, when Jeny's birthday was approaching, she had a definite idea about a certain present that she wanted. When my mom casually asked her, "What do you want for your birthday this year?" Jeny answered without any hesitation. "I want a tape recorder." Over the next few weeks, as her birthday came closer, she began to talk about it more and more. It consumed all of her thoughts for the last few weeks of her eleventh year on earth. She told everyone she knew that she wanted a tape recorder for her birthday. She told Mom and Dad. She told my sisters and me. She told all her friends, and she even told her friend's mother, Kay Hobart.

Kay Hobart was the kind of person who liked to tease and *get a rise* out of little kids. Kay told Jeny that tape recorders were expensive, and she doubted that Jeny would get one for her birthday. Jeny told Kay that she felt sure about it, because it was the only thing that she really, really wanted that year, and besides that, she had dropped so many hints that everyone knew.

Kay said, "I don't know... I don't think you'll get a tape recorder." Jeny started to simmer a little. Her voice got louder.

"Oh, I really think I will." Kay said, "Oh I don't think so… You'll probably just get a picture of a tape recorder. You won't get a real tape recorder." Jeny protested. "Oh you wanna make a bet. I'll bet you a million dollars." Kay said, "Oh Cripes… You don't have a million dollars." Jeny said, "I know, but I'll get a tape recorder. I'll prove it to you." Kay had a teasing smile on her face. Jeny was getting madder and madder. Jeny finally dropped her respectful speaking-to-an-adult voice, and switched over to her sandlot-arguing voice. "Kay Hobart, just you wait and see. I'll get a tape recorder for my birthday. Just you wait."

Jeny's birthday fell on a Saturday that year. When the big day rolled around, I awoke to the smell of angel food cake baking in the oven. My mom always baked angel food cake for every birthday. She had a special pan that was made just for the purpose. She called it the angel food cake baking pan. The shape of the pan caused the cake to have a big hole in the center. When the cake was finished, it looked like a giant donut with a flat top.

When Mom saw me entering the kitchen that morning, she told me to walk softly so the cake wouldn't fall. I'd never actually seen a fallen cake, but I sure heard a lot of warnings about them. I had a half notion to stomp my feet so I could actually see the cake fall, but as I weighed the pros and cons, I decided against it. I didn't want to risk losing out on a chance to lick the mixing beaters.

My mom said, "I thought you'd be up soon. I saved you the beaters." She read my mind, and I read hers. I guess you could say that my mom and I had a special understanding. She gave me cake beaters, and I tiptoed when there was a cake in the oven. It was an equitable arrangement.

When the cake was nearly finished baking, my mom pulled a long thin straw out of the corn broom that she used to sweep the kitchen floor. I don't know why they called it a corn broom. It was definitely not made out of corn or corn stalks or corn silk or corncobs or anything that looked like corn. It was made out of long strands of a yellowish dried plant material that resembled straw. She slid the oven shelf partway out, and then she stuck the clean end of the broom straw into the cake. She pushed that straw all the way to the bottom. When she pulled it back out again, she took a close look at the straw and said, "Hmm, I think it's done." I said, "How can you tell?" She said, "If the straw comes out clean, then the cake is keen." I took her word for it.

Mom turned off the oven and opened the drawer to get her giant pair of oven mitts. She said, "Now we have to let it cool for a while." She lifted the big cake pan up and out of the oven and carried it to the counter. Then, in one smooth motion, which she had perfected over years of practice, she turned the entire cake upside-down and placed the center hole onto the neck of a Pepsi bottle. Apparently, the hole in the center of the cake was there just for that purpose, and the special angel food cake pan hung in mid air, upside-down, on the bottle. It was a precarious looking contraption. My mom said, "Now you *really* have to tiptoe."

I always wondered, when my mom originally obtained that special angel food cake pan, if the Pepsi bottle came with it. I can picture the wording on the box in my mind: "Genuine

Angel Food Cake Pan. Perfect for making birthday cakes for every member of the family. Comes complete with an empty Pepsi bottle for precision upside down cake cooling."

Later, after it cooled, I watched my mom remove the cake from the pan. The top of the cake was brown and had big cracks and crevasses. My mom set the cracked side down and used the bottom side as the top. The bottom was much more pleasing to the eye and made a nice smooth surface for icing. (My mom never used frosting. It was always icing at the Utterback house.) My mom used her mixer once again and mixed up a nice batch of icing. I got to lick the beaters again. Icing beaters taste even better than cake beaters.

After the cake was iced, my mom asked me if I wanted to help her with the cake decorations. She unwrapped the little package of hard sugary cake decorations that she had bought from the grocery store. There were little flowers and curly-cues and alphabetic letters that spelled out "Happy Birthday." The decorations were stuck to a thick paper card. The instructions explained how to rub the back of the card with a wet cloth in order to loosen the decorations. After the little doodads were loose, my mom and I placed them on the top of the cake, and it became very festive looking.

We always kept a little box of birthday candles in the junk drawer. Mom told me I could have the honor of sticking twelve candles in the top of the cake. We used the same candles over and over for every birthday. They never burned down, because they were only lit long enough to sing the song; and it's a very short song.

Jeny's party began directly after the noon meal. The entire family was present: Mom, Dad, Debbie, Joyce, Jeny, Jeff, and Laura. Debbie, the oldest, was in her last year of high school and hadn't yet flown the coop. After the dishes had been cleared away, Mom grabbed a book of matches from the junk drawer, and the kitchen was filled with the smell of sulfur as she struck a match. My sister Laura immediately jumped up from the table and opened the drawer beneath the electric stove where Mom kept all of the saucepan lids. Laura grabbed a nice pair of lids in preparation for the singing of the birthday song. Over the years, Laura had instituted her own tradition of playing the cymbals during the song. When all eleven candles were glowing, my mom set the cake in front of Jeny, and we all began singing.

Happy Birthday to You, *clang*
Happy Birthday to You, *clang*
Happy Birthday dear Jeny, *clang*
Happy Birthday to You, *clang*

Jeny made her silent wish and promptly blew out all the candles in one breath.

Since Jeny was the birthday girl, she was honored with the duty of removing the candles and sucking the icing off the bottom of each one before dropping them back into the little candle box. I doubt if we ever washed those candles. They must have had many years worth of Utterback family slobber on them.

After the candles were removed, my mom leaned in and began to cut the cake over Jeny's shoulder. Mom was an angel food cake connoisseur. She wouldn't dream of using an ordinary knife. She used a very special device that some slick talking salesman had sold to her at the county fair. It was an angel food cake cutter. It had a black handle, and the business end had a series of thin stainless steel prongs hanging down. My mom plunged the prongs down deep into the cake, and then she sawed it back and forth. An ordinary knife tended to squash an angel food cake. This device was designed to avoid that problem. Apparently, it worked, or at least my mom thought it worked, because she always insisted on using it for every birthday.

After everyone in the family had enjoyed a piece of birthday cake, and after Laura and I had eaten our fill of those sugary birthday cake decorating doodads, it was time for the big present opening ceremony. My mom began to place several nicely wrapped presents on the table in front of Jeny, and Jeny began politely reading the cards and eagerly opening the presents. The first few boxes contained clothes. Jeny was old enough to know that it was her duty to smile and make appropriate comments. She said, "Oh very pretty," and then politely thanked the responsible party. She may have fooled Mom and Dad, but I could see her gritting her teeth every time she opened a box and found another shirt or a pair of culottes.

Near the end of the present pile, Jeny came upon a heavy one that seemed to be a likely candidate. It was about the right size and shape, and I saw a big batch of hope flash across her face. Jeny said, "I wonder what this could be," and I sensed a hush fall over the room as the family members paid close attention to this one. We all watched Jeny rip the pretty paper off. Jeny's face lit up and a huge smile emerged as she saw the wording on the box: Montgomery Ward, Portable Cassette

Tape Recorder. The box also had a big picture of the device and Jeny was ecstatic.

The unit was the size of a shoebox. It was black and came complete with a small hand held microphone and one sixty-minute blank cassette tape. After installing the batteries and reading the instructions, Jeny was ready to go. She pressed the play and record buttons simultaneously, then, speaking into the microphone, she introduced herself and prompted each family member to say something. First, my oldest sister Debbie spoke using her prim and proper voice. "Oh Hello. I am Deborah Jane Utterback." Then Jeny moved the microphone to Joyce, and she followed Debbie's lead but less formally. She said with a little giggle, "Hi I'm Joyce Utterback." My dad was sitting next to Joyce, and he was in one of his moods. He looked at the microphone that Jeny held in front of him, opened his mouth, and exhaled as if someone trying to fog up their glasses before cleaning them. There was some faint giggling in the room. My mom introduced herself next on the microphone, and then it was my turn. I used a goofy-sounding voice appropriate for a second-grader. Last but not least, Laura excitedly introduced herself. Speaking quickly and running her words together, she said, "I'm Laura Utterback." Forever after that day, when we played the tape back a hundred times, Jeny and I always insisted that she actually said, "I-want-my-water-back."

After all the introductions, Jeny started taking suggestions about what she should record next. Debbie was intently reading the instruction manual for the new tape recorder. She thought it would be a good idea to actually record someone reading the instructions in case they were ever lost. The next thing you hear on the tape is my sister Debbie using her most proper and studious straight-A student voice. "This Montgomery Ward model 34J portable monophonic cassette tape recorder is warranted against manufacturing defects and workmanship for a period of ninety days after the date of sale. Montgomery Ward will, at its discretion, repair or replace the unit if it fails to perform properly within the warranted period. With proper care and handling, this Montgomery Ward model 34J portable monophonic cassette tape recorder will function correctly for many years of service well beyond the warranty period."

Later in the day, Jeny was looking for other interesting things to record. I was itching to get my voice on there, and Jeny decided to give me a shot at greatness. I decided to tell my favorite knock-knock joke. I said, "Knock, knock" in a very goofy sounding voice, and you can hear Jeny in the background saying, "talk right," and then you can hear a click, and I begin again with a more serious delivery. I played both parts and answered myself during the knock-knock joke. "Knock, knock... Who's there? ... Moo... Moo who... Don't cry cow."

At another spot on the tape, you can hear my dad consoling Laura. "What's a matter Laura?" Laura answers sadly, "I didn't get to say anything." "You didn't get to say anything? Well what do you want to say?" "Anything." "Hmm?" "*Anything.*" "You wanna sing a song? Hmmm? How about *Three Blind Mice?*" My dad begins to sing, "Three blind mice... Three blind mice..." and you can hear Laura perking up to sing along with Dad. "See how they run... See how they run..." Then Laura takes over with the high part. "They all ran after the farmer's wife. She cut off their tails with a carving knife. Did you ever see such a site in your life as three blind mice."

As soon as the song ends, you can hear me chime in with a brilliant idea that had just occurred to me. Very loud and distorted you hear, "*TWO DEAD BOYS.*" Then my dad says, "ah, ah, ah, not so close, son. Back away from the microphone." Then the tape abruptly stops, and you can hear me begin again speaking simultaneously with Jeny. I guess we decided to do it together. We both spoke slowly and enunciated well.

> One bright day, in the middle of the night,
> Two dead boys got up to fight.
> Back to back, they faced each other,
> Drew their swords, and shot each other.
> The deaf policeman heard the noise,
> And came and got those two dead boys.
> If you don't believe this lie is true,
> Ask the blind man; he said it, oops, saw it too.

Jeny glared at me for making that mistake in the last line. I had to live with the mistake forever after and hear it again each time we played the tape back.

Later in the afternoon, Jeny was cooking up a plan to call Kay Hobart on the phone. Her plan was not to actually talk to Kay, but to play back a little speech from the tape recorder into the telephone. First, she had to record the speech on tape. Jeny warned me to keep quiet. She turned on the recorder, and I sat watching. I liked to watch the little spindles turning the tape when Jeny was recording. I also noticed a little red light on the tape recorder that glowed dimmer or brighter depending upon how loud you spoke into the microphone. It was a sort of recording level indicator. As Jeny started recording, I watched the little red light.

Jeny was using her I-told-you-so voice. "Kay Hobart. This is Jeny, and today is my birthday. I am calling to inform you that I did *not* receive just a picture of a tape recorder, but a real live tape recorder. In fact, you are now hearing me talking on the tape, if you can recognize the *SOUND OF MY VOICE!*" When Jeny said that, the little red light lit up very brightly, and I was amazed. I completely forgot my promise to remain quiet, and I exclaimed, "Wow! It lighted up really bright when you said that!" Jeny snapped her fingers at me and frowned and continued her speech. I felt bad, and when we played it back, you could hear that my statement was recorded onto the tape. Jeny was mad at me, but after she calmed down, she decided to go ahead with her plan. She called the Hobart house and asked for Kay. She pushed the play button and held the phone near the tape recorder. Kay listened to the speech, and then Jeny talked to Kay on the phone. Kay said, "Oh Cripes. You got a tape recorder. That's great!" Kay congratulated Jeny and told her to bring the tape recorder over to her house. She wanted to see it.

Jeny, Laura, and I walked over to the Hobart house. When we got there, Mike, Suzie, and Kay were home. Mike was about my age and Suzie was about Jeny's age. Laura was the odd man out, but she didn't mind. I always liked going to visit my friend Mike Hobart and Jeny considered Suzie to be a good friend. Jeny showed off her new tape recorder and played back the stuff that she had recorded so far. I had heard the tape played back so many times that I knew it all by heart. I knew the place where my dad exhaled into the mike, I knew the place where Laura said, "I want my water back," and I cringed when I heard myself say, "Wow, it lighted up really bright..."

Kay told Jeny about something that her oldest son, Johnnie, once did with a tape recorder. She said, "You oughta make a tape like Johnnie did," and then she explained it to us. We all thought it was a cool idea. Jeny and Suzie started looking for a suitable room to record in. They settled on using the master bedroom because it had the scariest sounding door hinge. Then Jeny started assigning parts to all the kids. Jeny and Suzie discussed the logistics, and then after all the plans were made, Jeny pressed the play and record button simultaneously.

The recording began with Jeny breathing heavily into the microphone in a slow and steady manor. "Huuu Haaaa." "Huuu Haaaa." After five or six of these heavy breathes, Jeny pointed at me to perform my assigned task. Very slowly, I swung the door to the bedroom open. The hinges made an excellent long and eerie creaking sound. After the sound was exhausted, Jeny continued her slow and heavy breathing as she pointed to Mike for him to begin his part. Mike, wearing his father's heavy welding shoes on his hands, proceeded to crawl across the wooden bedroom floor while clomping the heavy shoes. The clomping and the heavy breathing continued for another twenty seconds or so, and then Jeny gave the high-sign to Suzie. Suzie let loose with the longest and loudest and highest pitched girly scream I had ever heard in my entire life. I was very impressed, and a bit deafened. I had a crush on Suzie, and her incredible scream just deepened my admiration for her. Directly after the blood-curdling scream, Jeny indicated to Laura that she could do her part. Laura began cackling like a witch. "Yat, Yat, Yat, Yat, Yaaaaaah." At this point, Mike began his slow and deliberate clomping back to the bedroom door, and the heavy breathing accompanied him all along the way. I once again was directed to do my stuff with the door. The door hinges cooperated and once again produced a very long and creepy squeaking sound. The door finally came to a close with a small clunk, and then Jeny threw in one last "Huuu Haaaa" for good measure before stopping the tape.

We played it back over and over again. It sounded very good. We amazed ourselves. We pulled it off in one take. Kay Hobart was very impressed with our work, although it wasn't quite as good as Johnnie's. Every time I heard Suzie scream during the playback, I was even more impressed with her vocal abilities. It was an awarding-winning, blood-curdling, scream that could match up against anything that I had ever heard on the *Creature Feature* movies.

During the next several weeks, after Jeny's birthday, she dreamed up other interesting things to do with her tape recorder. She continued to add more items to the same blank tape. One time, Jeny coerced Laura and me to sing several songs with her on tape. We sang *Rain Drops Keep Falling on My Head*, the *Pepsi Generation* commercial, and also a few of the Partridge Family hits.

One day, I noticed the tape recorder in the bedroom where Jeny and Laura slept. I was alone in the house. Everyone was outside gardening or riding bikes or something. Nobody was around except for me. I couldn't resist the temptation. I rewound the tape and listened to the whole thing again for the umpteenth time. Then, I came to a part that I had never heard before. It was a secret part of the tape that Jeny had recorded in private.

She said rather shyly, "Um … this song is dedicated to … um … Steve Gather. I think you are so cute and so nice, and I hope you have a chance to hear this someday because I'm scared to tell you in person." Then she sang her song very slowly and seriously.

> Star light, star bright,
> Very first star I see tonight.
> I wish I may, I wish I might,
> Have the wish, I wish tonight.

After hearing Jeny's song, it put me in a sensitive mood. I was alone in the house, and I couldn't resist the temptation to record something of my own. I looked around the room for ideas. I saw Laura's coin bank on her dresser. The bank was in the shape of a tan colored Cocker Spaniel with a coin slot in his head. He was supposed to have a collar that said, "Sandy" but I had accidentally broken the collar several months prior. Laura cried about it, and I don't think I ever properly apologized. I decided to record an apology for Laura. I pushed the play and record buttons and began to speak the way Jeny had done it. "Um … this song is dedicated to … um … Laura. I'm sorry that I broke your dogs collar." Then I sang a short song, very slowly and seriously. It was in the slow and sensitive style that Donny Osmond used for his hit *Go Away Little Girl.*

> Sandy…
> I know you lost your collar…
> But Sandy…
> I know you won't holler…

A day or two later, after I had completely forgotten about it, Jeny came to me with a scowl on her face. She poked me in the chest and gritted her teeth and said, "Don't you ever touch my tape recorder. You got it, Buster?" I just nodded my head, and then she walked away.

As time went by, Jeny began using her tape recorder to record all the hits on her favorite radio station: WLS. She bought some new blank tapes for that purpose. She started spending a lot of time in her room waiting for them to play her favorite songs. She held the microphone up to the radio speaker, and she had to be very quite so that the tape wouldn't pick up any noise in the room. If anyone walked in and started talking, she'd get very upset. I know that Mom got scolded several times for barging in with the clean laundry right in the middle of a recording session.

Jeny started keeping a notebook with information about which tape contained which hit song and where on the tape it could be found. There was a counter on the tape recorder. She could fast-forward and watch the counter and start playing the song when the counter came to the proper place.

One time Jeny wanted to test her record keeping ability. She asked me to perform an independent test. She told me to look at the notebook and request one of the songs, and she'd play it for me. After several minutes of looking, I couldn't find the song I wanted to hear. Jeny was getting impatient with me. Finally she said, "Well just tell me what you wanna hear, and I'll tell you if I have it." I told her I wanted to hear, "Bathroom on the Right." She said, "*Bathroom on the Right? There is no such song!*" I said, "Yes there is. They play it all the time on WLS." She said, "I never heard of it! Sing it for me." I began to sing.

Aw, don't go out tonight.

Because everything will be all right.

Theeeere's a bathroom on the right.

Jeny laughed and said, "You are so dumb! There's a *Bad Moon on the Rise*! You weirdo!" Then she looked at her list and found the song and loaded in the appropriate tape and fast-forwarded to the proper count and played the song for me. It was a successful test.

Once in a while, Jeny would get a new idea to use up a little more of that original blank tape that came with the tape recorder. One time she pretended to be a female radio personality on station "WBLB Blab." She interviewed my sister Joyce about high school. "Good afternoon everyone. Today on station WBLB Blab, we are going to interview Miss Joyce Utterback about the school she attends."

"Now, uh, Miss Utterback … does your school have a name?"

"Oh yes of course. It's PTHS."

"Oh I see PTHS … and does that stand for something?"

"Oh yes of course. It stands for Pontiac Township High School."

"Oh I see, Pontiac Township High School. Yes, I believe I have heard of that one."

"Now, uh, Miss Utterback … does your school have a sports mascot?"

"Oh yes of course. We are the Indians, and our basketball team was great last year. They went all the way to the district finals or something like that."

"Oh I see, the district finals. That's good … I think."

"Now, uh, Miss Utterback … do you have a favorite subject?"

"Well … Home-Ec, I guess."

"Oh I see, and do you like your Home-Ec teacher?"

"Oh yes of course, Miss Hesterberg. She's just the belle of the ball."

"Oh I see … what was that term you used: belle of the ball?"

"Oh yes of course. She's the best teacher we've got."

"Oh I see … the belle of the ball. I'll make a note of that."

At this point, Jeny decided it was time for a commercial break. "Now I'm afraid that it's time for a break here on station WBLB Blab on your radio dial. Don't touch that dial. We'll be right back on station WBLB Blab." Jeny started singing the Pepsi song and prompted Joyce to join her on the ending, then the interview continued. "OK, we're back on station WBLB Blab on your radio dial. Today, we are speaking with Miss Joyce Utterback about the high school she attends."

"Now, uh, Miss Utterback … does your school have a Prom?"

"Oh yes of course. I think all high schools have a Prom, except for the little icky ones like Flanagan."

(The news reporter begins to cough and sputter.)

"Oh (cough, cough) well we don't want to insult anyone, now do we?"

"Now, uh, Miss Utterback … does your school have a yearly musical performance?"

"Oh yes of course. Last year we did *West Side Story,* and I was in it."

"Oh I see … and did you have a good part?"

"Well … I guess so. I was a Puerto Rican."

"Oh I see … a Puerto Rican … and did you have a lot of lines?"

"Well … no … but I got to paint my face brown and sing with all the other Puerto Ricans."

"Oh I see."

"Now, uh, Miss Utterback ... do you have a dress code at your
   high school?"

"Oh no, not now! They just got rid of the dress code last year!
   Everybody is so happy about it! You can wear what ever
   you want! ... Well not what *ever* you want, but you know
   what I mean."

"Oh I see ... that sounds great ... and can you wear culottes?"

"Well ... I suppose so ... but I don't know anyone who'd *want* to."

After the interview was over, the original blank tape was
nearly used up. It contained a full hours-worth of wonderful
Utterback family memories. Jeny was so creative and full of
fun ideas. She really had a good time with her tape recorder.
Laura and I never got tired of hearing that tape played back
over and over again. During one of the playbacks, at the place
where Jeny sings *Star Light Star Bright,* I noticed that the name
of Steve Gather had been emphatically changed to, "*Nobody In
Particular!*"

CB Radio: A National Phenomenon

~~~~~~

During the mid 1970s, a strange fad took hold of America. People started using strange words and calling themselves by strange names and holding long conversations with complete strangers. It began with the truck drivers but soon jumped to the ordinary people like a virus jumps from one species to another. The fad passed quickly over the entire U.S.A. and became a national phenomenon. It was called Citizen's Band or CB for short. Every truck driver had a CB radio, and then the farmers began installing them in their tractors and their pickup-trucks. After that, ordinary people began installing CBs in their cars and houses, and before long, nearly everyone in the entire country had a CB radio. Doctors and lawyers, factory workers and housewives, teenagers and grandpas all began speaking over the airwaves using a strange offshoot of the English language.

I wanted to jump on the CB bandwagon, but the cost of a CB radio was out of my league. My parents were frugal and cautious. It took a few years before my dad broke down and bought one. In the mean time, I had a set of toy walkie-talkies and that satisfied my desire to send my voice through the air.

Sometimes when playing with my walkie-talkies, I could hear unfamiliar voices and faint conversations that faded in and out. "Break. Break. Break. How bout it skip-land, skip-land, skip-land. Woooo! You got the Red Rooster here outa southern California. Mercy, mercy! How bout it. Come on back." When I tried to respond, he couldn't hear me, so I gave up and just resorted to listening. My friend, Myron Burton, was familiar with CB radios because his dad was a truck driver. Myron told me that Red Rooster probably had an illegal CB with a lot of power and a huge antenna. He was *skipping* his signal off the atmosphere. "They call it skip-land," Myron told me.

If Red Rooster had a CB, and I had a toy walkie-talkie, I wondered why I could hear that guy. Myron solved the mystery when he read the fine print on the back of my walkie-talkie. "This True-Value True-Tone Walkie-Talkie operates on Citizen's Band channel 14 and conforms to all known FCC regulations defined for a low power recreational communication device." That was a fortunate thing for me. I could participate in the national CB craze as long as everyone I knew stayed on channel 14. Myron and I performed a little experiment. He jumped into the cab of his dad's truck and turned the CB to channel 14. Sure enough it worked. I was able to talk to Myron as long as we were within range of my low power walkie-talkie.

There was an unwritten rule that you couldn't use your real name when talking over the airwaves. I never quite understood why, but Myron gave me the impression that it was almost a criminal offense. All of the CB users had a *handle* that they used. Myron's father was known as *Cat*, and Myron was *Little Cat*. Myron's dad had a habit of using 1950's beatnik slang. He'd say things like, "What are you cats up to today?" I figured that's how he got his handle.

The Weber family, who lived in Swygert, also had CB radios. They had a powerful base station in the house. I think Mrs. Weber monitored channel 9, the emergency channel. She was a REACT volunteer. (Radio Emergency Associated Communication Team) Mr. Weber had a CB in his car, and he had a slightly risqué handle: *Horny Toad.*

My very favorite handle belonged to my friend's dad, Junior Hobart. Junior was a mild-mannered, easygoing type of guy. He never raised his voice. He was rather thin and always looked like he could use a shave. His wife, Kay, made up a CB handle for Junior. She called him *Hungry Eye.*

My friend, Dale Cagley, noticed all the fun I was having with my walkie-talkies. He desperately wanted to get in on the action. There were no CB radios in his family, but he scraped together his birthday money and bought a walkie-talkie similar to mine. Actually, Dale's walkie-talkie was a step or two better than mine. He didn't buy a set of walkie-talkies; he just bought one. It had several more knobs and switches than mine had. It even had a *squelch!*

Dale's walkie-talkie had a special switch on the front panel that said, "Chan-A Chan-B." When the switch was on Chan-A, I could talk to him just fine. When the switch was on Chan-B, I couldn't. We were showing off Dale's new walkie-talkie all around Swygert when we ran into Mr. Weber. Dale asked him about his Chan-B switch. We knew that Chan-A was channel 14, but we couldn't figure out Chan-B. Mr. Weber opened up his car door and turned on his CB. He told Dale to say something so he could hunt through the channels in hopes of finding out which channel Chan-B was broadcasting on.

Dale didn't know what to say. He was struck with a case of stage fright. We all coaxed him to talk. Dale was nervous about talking to an adult. He wanted to make sure he used the correct CB language. Mr. Weber didn't care what he said as long as he said something. Dale finally found some words in his memory that he thought would be appropriate. He pushed the button and said, "Hey Horny Toad, you got a copy?" Mr. Weber shook his head and told him to keep talking. Dale pushed the button again and said, "Hey Horny Toad, you got a copy? Hey Horny Toad, you got a copy? Hey Horny Toad, you got a copy? Hey Horny Toad, you got a copy?" This went on and on for five minutes while Mr. Weber clicked through each of the possible CB channels. Mrs. Weber came out on the porch to see what was happening. She said, "Dale, it sounds like your needle is stuck in the groove."

Mr. Weber never did *get a copy* on any of the channels. A couple days later, Dale told me that he had finally read the instructions. It said Chan-B wouldn't work unless he bought a crystal: sold separately. Dale decided just to be satisfied with Chan-A. My dad taught me to be an avid instruction reader, so I was appalled that Dale had been using his walkie-talkie for two days without reading the instructions.

As time went on, everyone in Swygert jumped on the CB bandwagon. The Hobarts ended up with two or three of them, and my dad eventually bought a CB radio as well. After that, I was no longer limited to channel 14. I could listen to the truckers on channel 19. "Breaker one nine, we got us a smokey takin' pictures up at marker one nine seven on the double nickle." "Ten-roger ... good on ya ... mercy sakes ... better back 'em down."

Giant Closets and
Halloween Parties

The upper level of our two-story house had two bedrooms, a full bathroom, and a giant hallway. At least, we always called it a hallway. It was actually a strange open room that you had to cross through in order to get to Debbie's room. The hallway was so big that it held a full-size single bed, a bookcase, and sometimes also a baby crib. Since there were five kids in my family, the big hallway came in handy. For several years, the hallway served as my bedroom. I enjoyed it very much until I got a chance to move into Joyce's room, after she left the nest.

The big hallway also had another unique feature. It contained a huge, built-in, floor to ceiling closet. There were three big closet doors side by side. Each one was about three feet wide and six feet high. Above the three main doors, there were three smaller cubbyholes up near the ceiling. Each cubbyhole also had a door. The closet is what most people would call a handyman special. It looked like it had been constructed by an amateur carpenter on a strict budget. The doors were made out of thin plywood, and were held closed with a cheap metal catch. Some of the doors were warped, the catch didn't always catch, and one of the doors always stood a few inches ajar. The U-shaped wooden door handles were also homemade, and the whole closet was painted a yellowish-greenish color.

One time, when playing hide-n-seek, I discovered a cool trick. I found that I could actually crawl into the closet, crawl over the shoes and boxes, crawl under the clothes hanging on the rod and come out in Debbie's room. The back of her closet was actually connected to the big hallway closet. When I figured this out, I kept it a secret. I thought it might come in handy sometime. I assumed that I was the only person in the world who knew about this cool trick. It reminded me of those old mansions on the TV horror movies that had a secret passage way.

I have very fond memories of that big closet. The contents of the center door became very important to me somewhere near Halloween when I was in the first-grade at Owego School. The closet turned out to be a bonanza of great Halloween costume ideas.

Owego School had a well-established Halloween tradition. Every year, the school held a Halloween Party in the gym. The party was always hosted by the PTA. It was held on some convenient night near Halloween, but not usually on October 31. On the way to the party, we'd sometimes give a ride to Jeny's friend, Ruth Pennington. Ruth was in Jeny's class, and four years older than me. She was very pretty except for one eyetooth that sort of stuck out. One Halloween, Ruth wore a little brown Indian squaw costume with fringe at the bottom that hit her just about mid thigh. Most people think that girls have no effect upon first-grade boys, but I assure you that they do.

The kids and parents would usually arrive for the party around 7:00 PM. The kids always arrived with their costumes on. After entering the gym, the kids would begin pacing up and down the gym floor. If your costume was very clever, and you kept your mouth shut, it might take two or three paces up and down the floor before the other kids could figure out who you were. This pacing seems a strange tradition to me now, but it was perfectly normal back then, and all the kids did it. It was a sort of indoor Halloween parade I guess.

After the latecomers had a chance to arrive, the big costume contest would begin. The PTA always managed to dig up someone to act as an impartial costume judge. Some years the costume judge actually dressed up in a costume just to join in with the fun. It was an unwritten rule that if you showed up in a store-bought costume, you wouldn't win. The judges seemed to favor originality, craftsmanship, and good country costume making know-how.

The big closet was a wonderful thing for anyone seeking an original Halloween costume. Each year around Halloween time, my mom would escort me to the big closet to see what we could find. I had a great advantage with the fact that three older siblings had also gone to Owego School, so there was a vast assortment of hand-me-down Halloween stuff to choose from. There was a wonderful smell when opening the closet door. The smell was like a mix of fresh sheets and old tablecloths and musty jigsaw puzzles and my sister's clarinet case and my fathers Korean Conflict Army uniform. As we looked through the closet, we found a treasure trove of Halloween odds and ends. There was a bright yellow wig with a female hobo mask. There was a big red clown nose and some big clown shoes. There was a Dennis the Menace mask with a matching toy slingshot. There was an authentic old grandma wig with plenty of gray hair tied up in a tight bun. Besides all that, there were countless other odds and ends: hippie beads, a stovepipe hat, a bloody doctors apron, and a pair of matching green plastic witch masks complete with a wart on each nose.

Every year my sisters and I would make it a point to watch *The Charlie Brown Halloween Special* on TV. It usually aired a few days before Halloween. We'd rather die than miss watching the show each year. It was always sponsored by Dolly Madison Zingers. I liked the part where Charlie Brown got a little overzealous with the scissors and his ghost outfit ended up with ten or twenty eye-holes. I always loved the way Charlie Brown's Jack-o'-Lantern looked. The mouth was a sort of zigzag. I thought that zigzag mouth was really great. Every year, when we carved our family Jack-o'-Lantern, I always wanted it to have a zigzag mouth just like Charlie Brown's.

One year we actually grew pumpkins in our vegetable garden for the purpose of making a Halloween Jack-o'-Lantern. The pumpkin plant had no respect for the nice neat garden rows that my parents created. It sent its vines out anywhere it liked. We had pumpkins growing among the onions and invading into the green beans. The pumpkin plant completely ignored the boundary of the garden and sent a couple of long tentacles out into the yard.

The first time I learned how to carve a Jack-o'-Lantern, I watched my mom cut a nice big hole in the cranium, and then she asked me to help her pull out the guts. It was dark inside there, and I saw a mess of stringy, gooey, yucky stuff. I didn't want to stick my hand in there, but my mom showed me there was nothing to be afraid of. I soon learned to fearlessly plunge my whole arm in and pull out those guts. My mom told me to save the pumpkin seeds. She spread them out on a cookie sheet, added a little salt, and then she roasted them in the oven. I never became a big fan of roasted pumpkin seeds, but I always tried a few of them every year just for the sake of tradition.

Several days before Halloween, I'd set our Jack-o'-Lantern outside on the planter ledge. I always wanted to light it after supper so that it would glow for all the passing cars to see. Every year, on our way to the Owego Halloween Party, my mom allowed me to light the Jack-o'-Lantern so that it could greet us with its flickering zigzag smile when we got back home.

Somewhere around fourth-grade, I decided to be a mad scientist for Halloween. The bloody doctor's smock from the big closet came in handy, and I also wore a plastic stethoscope from my sister's toy doctor kit. My mom used scraps from an old bed sheet to make a lovely white surgical mask to cover my mouth and nose. I used a floor mop for a wig, sans mop handle, and I wore a giant pair of black plastic glasses. The thing that really finished off my outfit was that I carried a big old rusty pipe-wrench from my dad's toolbox, and a well-worn pair of giant tin-snips. The tin-snips looked like a humongous pair of industrial strength scissors. I thought it was just the kind of tool that a mad scientist would use. Whenever I felt the urge, I'd clank my tin-snips and pipe-wrench together for some sound effects.

When it came time for the Owego School costume contest, I climbed the three steps from the gym floor to the stage with my fingers mentally crossed. I had never won the contest before, and I really wanted to win this year. I had put a lot of effort into my costume, and I thought that I had a chance of winning. I stood facing outward with the other kids in my group. We all waited patiently as the costume judge considered the ghouls and goblins before her.

As the judge carefully looked over the costumes, I waited about a half-minute, and then I strategically clanked my big tools together for effect. I think that did the trick, because I won the contest that year. My prize was a giant candy-bar or some such thing. I was very happy, but I tried not to gloat. My parents had spent a lot of time teaching me how to be a good sport. I put my giant candy-bar over next to my mom's purse to save it for later.

Each year, while the costume contest was in progress, other members of the PTA were busily setting up the cupcakes, cookies, and Kool-Aid. After the contest, everyone would sit down and take a rest and enjoy the lovely refreshments. I always wondered who invented cupcakes. They're just perfect for such an event. No utensils necessary. I could easily eat two and maybe casually go back again to take a third, but I never dared to try for four. I was afraid that someone would notice, and then I'd have the reputation of being a pig.

Somewhere around 8:00 or 8:30 PM, the games would begin. Each year some clever PTA member would try to come up with some new kind of game to play.

- Run to the other end of the gym, sit on a balloon, and run back so the next kid can go.

- Carry a peanut on a spoon down to the other end of the gym, drop the peanut in a bucket, and run back so the next kid can go.

- Drop a clothespin into a milk bottle, then get out of the way so the next kid can go. (No bending over allowed.)

In addition to those games, there was always the classic, Pin the Tail on the Donkey. No matter what precautions those PTA ladies would take, some kid always found a way to peek through the blindfold.

After all the fun and games were over, and I had worn myself to a frazzle running back and forth across the gym floor with a peanut on my spoon, it would be time for the party to end. It was always a sad time. I never wanted it to end. I'd say goodbye to my friends, and my mom would say something like, "My goodness, how did you get so sweaty?" When we'd leave the gym, the cool October night air would hit me in the face, and it would feel so good. I'd hear some farmer in the distance running his tractor at night. The farmers wouldn't let a little thing like darkness stop them from harvesting. When the corn was ready, it was ready.

As my mom was driving my sisters and I home, she'd ask, "Was that fun?" and we'd all say yes. I'd hear my little sister rustling with candy wrappers in the back seat, then I'd smell the smell of Bazooka Bubble Gum as she popped a piece into her mouth. When we got home, I'd smell the corn dust in the air, and I'd hear the steady drone of the grain dryers running at the grain elevator across the road. I'd also see that all the lights were on at the elevator office. The elevator stayed open late at night during harvest season. I'd see my Jack-o'-Lantern glowing dimly. I'd grab the stem, open the cranium, and blow out the candle. Another wonderful Owego School Halloween Party had ended, and I'd treasure the memory forever.

Made in the USA
Monee, IL
17 December 2021